CRAZY HORSE

WAR CHIEF OF THE OGALA SIOUX

To my brother, Ken Goldman—
a dedicated teacher and a very creative writer.

M. S. G.

Map (p. 12) by Gary Tong
Photographs copyright ©: New York Public Library Picture Collection: pp. 14, 154; U.S. Signal Corps, National Archives: pp. 16, 44, 116; National Collection of Fine Arts, Smithsonian Institution: p. 26; Wyoming Department of Commerce, Division of Cultural Resources: p. 32; North Wind Picture Archives: pp. 53, 150; Smithsonian Institution: p. 60; Smithsonian Office of Anthropology, Bureau of American Ethnology Collection: p. 74; State Historical Society of North Dakota: p. 93; Archive Photos: pp. 104, 121; Denver Public Library, Western History Department: pp. 113, 137; Detroit Public Library: p. 131; Burlington Northern Railroad Photo Archives: p. 142; Southwest Parks and Monuments Association: p. 158; Nebraska State Historical Society: pp. 167, 175; University of Nebraska Press: p. 174; UPI/Bettmann: p. 183.

Library of Congress Cataloging-in-Publication Data
Goldman, Martin S.
    Crazy Horse : war chief of the Oglala Sioux / by Martin S. Goldman.
    p. cm. — (The American Indian Experience) Includes bibliographical references and index.
    Summary: A biography of the Sioux leader set against the history of the Indian wars, with a full account of the Battle of the Little Bighorn.
    ISBN 0-531-11258-6
    1. Crazy Horse, ca. 1842–1877—Juvenile literature. 2. Oglala Indians—Biography—Juvenile literature. 3. Oglala Indians—Wars—Juvenile literature. 4. Little Bighorn, Battle of the, Mont., 1876—Juvenile literature. [1. Crazy Horse, ca. 1842–1877. 2. Oglala Indians—Biography. 3. Indians of North America–Biography. 4. Little Bighorn, Battle of the, Mont., 1876.] I. Title. II. Series.
E99.03C72218   1996
978′.004975′0092—dc20   CIP AC
[8]   95-26412

CRAZY HORSE

WAR CHIEF OF THE OGLALA SIOUX

by MARTIN S. GOLDMAN

The American Indian Experience

FRANKLIN WATTS
A Division of Grolier Publishing
New York • London • Hong Kong • Sydney • Danbury, Connecticut

CONTENTS

ACKNOWLEDGMENTS

Crazy Horse: War Chief of the Oglala Sioux is the third book in a trilogy begun in 1992: the others are *Nat Turner and the Southampton Revolt of 1831* (New York: Franklin Watts, 1992) and *John F. Kennedy: Portrait of a President* (New York: Facts on File, 1995).

There is a common thread that runs through these studies and links the subjects, in my mind, in a historical sense: three very different young leaders of their people, caught up in the powerful forces of history which they did not understand and could not control; and all three, because of these forces, doomed to an early, tragic, and violent death.

A black slave, a patrician Irish-Catholic president, and a Native American warrior. I have attempted to re-create the times in which these men lived in order to show them set into a vast historical tapestry—of which we all are a part. As John Donne said, "No man is an island . . . " Thus, I am saying to students that it is as important to understand the times in which they lived as well as the human beings.

To me, the most compelling of the three leaders was Crazy Horse. He was an endlessly fascinating man and has pushed his way into my private dreams and visions. I would have liked to meet him. It is my hope that, in a small way, this study will create that meeting for the reader. It is not difficult to understand how, over sixty years ago, the writer Mari Sandoz was haunted by her "Strange Man." Anyone who attempts to ride the vast prairies of the Great Plains with the Sioux and with Crazy Horse owes much to Mari Sandoz. Without her work, Crazy Horse may have been consigned to a footnote in Custeriana and largely forgotten by everyone except the Sioux.

There are many debts for this book and many people who have helped along the trail. Foremost is Michael Kort, who teaches and writes history at Boston University. Mike has been a great friend, my *kemo sabe* (trusted scout), whose positive criticism and encouragement have always been vital, helpful, and unerringly valid. Without his support and friendship, and that of his wife, Carol Kort, there may well have been no trilogy.

To Lorna Greenberg, my editor at Franklin Watts, whose patience and editing skills have seen me through two books, many thanks. Lorna has the fastest (and most accurate) blue pencil in the West (as well as the North, South, and East).

To Ann Marchette, for an endless supply of coffee, bagels, and love—my gratitude for being part of my life.

To Gideon, the newest member of my Sudbury family, who patiently waited for his puppy chow while I tapped the computer in my quiet study and, when I got up, tore for the kitchen as if the house were on fire.

And to my two Larrys, Larry Lowenthal in Boston and Larry Laster in Philadelphia: you guys are what friendship is all about.

Finally, to my very supportive family—my parents, Louis and Ruth Goldman, my aunt Nan Praisman, and my brother, Ken Goldman—this book is dedicated to you.

M. S. G.

INTRODUCTION

People who find themselves at the juncture of worlds passing and worlds coming tend to be crushed like insects. —Henry Adams

Crazy Horse, one of the great Native American leaders, has been largely overlooked in the teaching and writing of American history. When he is remembered, the Sioux war chief is usually relegated to a few isolated paragraphs in references to the overwhelming defeat suffered by George Armstrong Custer at the Battle of the Little Bighorn in 1876.

A widely used college history text in the 1950s and 1960s noted,

> *Under Sitting Bull and Crazy Horse the Sioux struck back. In June 1876 they ambushed the impetuous "glory hunter," General [sic] George Armstrong Custer on the Little Bighorn, and annihilated his whole command of 264 men.... Punishment was swift; the Sioux were scattered and Crazy Horse captured and murdered by his guard.*[1]

Twenty years later the Sioux chieftain fared little better. In an American history text specifically designed to include women, African-Americans, and other minorities (as well as the untold story of the American Indian), a committee of authors made little improvement in their analysis of Crazy Horse's role in America's complex past. The Sioux had rebelled after a combination of events: a series of broken federal treaties allowing thousands of miners to search for gold on the Sioux lands in the Dakota territory, and the encroaching construction of the Northern Pacific Railroad.

Pointing to the uprising in their new text, the authors wrote,

> The revolt, led by Chiefs Rain-in-the-Face, Sitting Bull, and Crazy Horse, peaked June 26, 1876, when 2,500 braves annihilated the troops of the rash General [sic] George S. [sic] Custer near the Little Big Horn River in southern Montana. . . . By fall 1877, the Sioux war was over and other attempts at resistance had been quelled. . . . Crazy Horse had been murdered by soldiers while imprisoned in an army fort.[2]

Over the last century, Crazy Horse's brief life has been an inspiration to many Native Americans. His people, the Oglala Sioux, revere his name and memory. They remember one of their greatest chieftains in a manner similar to the way many Americans remember Founders such as George Washington and Thomas Jefferson, or Abraham Lincoln, the martyred president who led the Union during the Civil War and whose own paternal grandfather had been killed by an Indian while clearing a field in the early 1780s in Kentucky.[3]

Still, the historical record is very limited. To recapture the tumultuous era in which Crazy Horse lived, roughly the mid-nineteenth century, the reader must first understand that for the most part, Native Americans left no written historical record. With the exception of the Cherokees, who had developed an alphabet and their own newspapers, Indian history was passed from generation to generation largely by the spoken word. Many observations of Indian life came from the interpretation and writings of whites. Thus, to reconstruct the world of Crazy Horse, we must first view the American Indian through the prism of the painful relationship between Indians and whites in America's past. Then, we must finally attempt to understand how the American Indians have viewed themselves.

Most historians agree that it is impossible to pinpoint the exact time and place when Indians and whites first met. As one historian writes, "It is difficult to say of any recorded 'contact' (between Indians and whites) that it was indeed the first."[4]

However, we do know that the first explorers to the New World were generally welcomed peacefully by the natives with whom they came in contact. Christopher Columbus reported that he and his men were received openly and kindly by the first native inhabitants of the West Indian islands they met in October of 1492.

As Columbus recorded meeting Indians in his journals,

They all go naked as their mothers bore them. . . . They should be good servants and of quick intelligence, since I see that they very soon say all that is said to them, and I believe that they would easily be made Christians. . . .[5]

However, by the nineteenth century relations between Indians and whites had tragically deteriorated into an ongoing drama of broken promises, broken treaties, and broken dreams. One tribe after another was decimated by diseases such as smallpox and influenza, or by the overwhelming military might of the Spanish, French, and English in the colonial period, and then by the advancing westward movement of Americans in the years following the American Revolution.

Thus, before we can reconstruct Sioux life on the Great Plains and study the elusive and mystical war chief Crazy Horse, we must briefly analyze Indian–White relations in

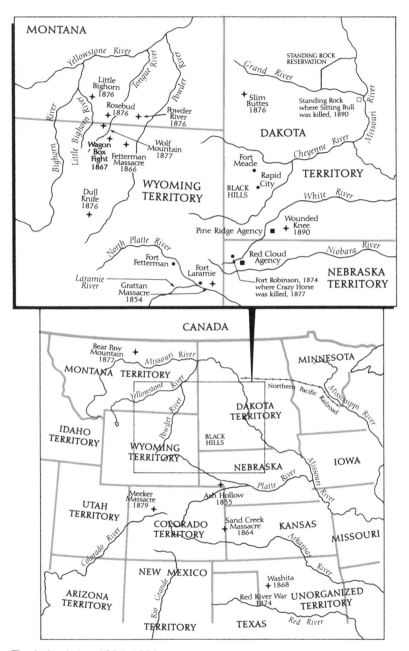

The Indian Wars 1854–1890
(The map at the top is an enlargement of the area indicated by the box on the lower map.)

the United States. The essential conflict between Native Americans and Europeans, and later, Americans, can be understood along two major fronts: culture and geography.

First, Indians were different from Europeans. Even though many settlers grew up in the wilderness or on the frontier, the essential cultural influence on the early colonists was English. As Winthrop D. Jordan has observed in his pathmark study on American racial attitudes, "Inevitably, the savagery of the Indians assumed a special significance in the minds of those actively engaged in a program of bringing civilization into the American wilderness."[6]

From the very beginning, the English viewed Native Americans as a distinct and dangerous entity blocking the advance of their culture and civilization. Winthrop D. Jordan saw that difference in terms of race. Jordan wrote, "Only with Indians and Negroes did Englishmen attempt so radical a deprivation of liberty." Thus, he asked "the most difficult and imponderable question of all":

What was it about Indians and Negroes which set them apart, which rendered them different from Englishmen, which made them special candidates for degradation?[7]

Finally, there was the land. The Indians had it in great abundance. The Europeans, and later their American descendants, wanted it.

In a picture drawn by an Indian eyewitness, Crazy Horse, wearing his protective hailstone medicine paint, and holding his Winchester rifle, rides his light-colored horse in pursuit of several U.S. cavalrymen at the Battle of the Little Bighorn, June 1876.

CHAPTER ONE

EARLY LIFE

In the fall of 1841, a Brulé Sioux woman gave birth to her second child, her first son, near a stream called Rapid Creek in the Black Hills of what is today South Dakota. She was the wife of the Oglala Sioux holy man called Crazy Horse.[1]

The child was different from most Oglala children. He was fair-skinned and had light, curly hair. Since it was Oglala custom not to name a man-child until he had earned his name by a heroic deed or a mystical experience as in a dream, his tribe gave him various nicknames related to his physical characteristics: "Curly Hair," and "Light-Haired Boy." But as the child grew into adolescence he was most often called "Curly."[2]

There were many branches of the Indian tribe known as "the Sioux." The Teton Sioux was a loose confederation of seven tribal groupings: the Oglala ("Scatters Their Own"); Brulé ("Burned Thighs"); Hunkpapa ("Campers at the Opening of the Circle"); Minniconjou ("Planters by Water"); Sans Arc ("Without Bows"); Two Kettle ("Two Boilings"); and Sihasapa ("Blackfeet"). Each of these tribes broke down further into little bands and groups. The Teton Sioux were the westernmost and largest of the groups that made up the tribe's Seven Council Fires. Far to the east of the Teton Sioux lived their cousins of the Santee grouping of the Sioux

The calm before the storm: a Sioux Indian tribe camps along the Laramie River, Wyoming Territory, in the early 1870s.

nation. Between these were the two remaining groups of Sioux, the Yankton and Yanktoni. The Teton, Santee, and Yankton branch called themselves Lakota, Dakota, and Nakota Sioux. The word *Sioux* itself was given to the tribe by their enemies to the east, who called them "nadouesis-siw," or "small snake." The French shortened that name to Sioux, which loosely translated meant "enemy."[3]

At one time all the Sioux tribes ranged in the wooded areas surrounding the headwaters of the Mississippi River. But by 1775 only the Santee Sioux still lived in the forests. The Sioux had begun the long trek westward as a result of incessant warfare with their traditional enemy, the Chippewa. The Chippewa, with access to firearms bought or traded from whites, had beaten the Sioux in battle on many occasions over the years. Thus, the Sioux had decided to migrate from their original homelands in what is today Minnesota.[4]

The Sioux found their way to the Great Plains—a vast region of flat, grassy prairie west of the Mississippi River that is treeless and semiarid (the rainfall is insufficient to provide for intensive agriculture). It is a large area of varied climate and intense weather patterns: strong winds, raging hailstorms, violent tornadoes, hot summers and cold winters.

Two things changed the Sioux way of life as various tribes migrated west: the horse and the buffalo. It is impossible to overestimate the effect of the horse on Indian life on the Great Plains. As Walter Prescott Webb wrote, "overnight . . . the whole life and economy of the Plains Indian was changed."[5]

The horse was introduced into the Americas by the Spanish explorer Hernán Cortés in the sixteenth century. The Spanish had used the horse in the military reconquest of Spain against the Turks and Moors. Cortés brought sixteen horses across the Atlantic when he landed in Mexico in 1519.[6] Eventually the Spanish horse herds multiplied, escaped, or were sat free by Indian raiders. Soon the Indian tribes inhabiting the Great Plains region taught themselves to ride. The Kiowa and Missouri Indians were mounted by 1682, the Pawnee by 1700, the Comanche, the most superb riders of all the Plains Indians, by 1714, and the Teton Sioux by 1742.[7]

By the time the Sioux moved west to the Great Plains, the horse had changed their way of life as well as their economy. Edward Lazarus notes, "By the eighteenth century, these ponies, rarely more than fourteen hands high but remarkable for their agility and endurance, numbered in the millions. The pintos gave the Sioux undreamed-of mobility and speed, and rapidly became indispensable to their hunting, warring, and roaming." The number of horses in a warrior's herd became the measure of his wealth and stature in the tribe. Stealing horses from other tribes was seen as honorable and quickly became part of Indian life on the Great Plains.[8]

However, by the time the Plains Indians had developed their equestrian (horse) culture, Indian life and culture in North and South America had been largely destroyed by white settlement. By the early to mid-nineteenth century, the Indian tribes of the East, who lived in semipermanent agricultural village settings, had been decimated. These tribes were not nomadic and had great difficulty adjusting to the West, where many of them were forced to move.[9]

If the horse gave the Great Plains tribes mobility, the buffalo, or American bison, gave them sustenance. A full-grown male buffalo weighed in at nearly a ton and a half and provided an enormous supply of meat. Sometimes a herd of buffalo extended across the Great Plains as far as the eye could see. One early Texas cowboy reported seeing a herd of 500,000 that stretched over fifty miles. The vast buffalo herds that lumbered clumsily across the Great Plains were said to number over seventy-five million. One observer reported to the Smithsonian Museum of Natural History in 1887, "It would have been as easy to count or estimate the number of leaves in a forest as to calculate the number of buffaloes living at any given time during the history of the species previous to 1870."[10]

Because the buffalo moved slowly and clumsily unless aroused, had poor eyesight and bad hearing, the great beasts were easy hunting for the Indians, who maneuvered through the large herds on fast buffalo ponies, with bow and arrow, and later, with guns, at their sides. The buffalo dominated every facet of Indian life and economy on the plains. George Catlin, an American artist who roamed the West in the 1830s, painting Indian scenes, noted in his jounal how important the buffalo was to the Indians of the Plains.

There are, by fair calculation, more than 300,000 Indians who are now subsisting on the flesh of the buffaloes, and by these animals supplied with all the luxuries of life which they desire, as they know of none others. . . . Every part of the flesh is converted into food, in one shape or another, and on it they entirely subsist. The robes of the animal are worn by the Indians instead of blankets; their skins when tanned are used as coverings for their lodges and for their beds; undressed [the skins] are used for constructing canoes, for saddles, for bridles, lariats, lassos and thongs. The horns are shaped into ladles and spoons . . . their bones are used for saddle trees, for war clubs, and scrapers for graining the robes, and others are broken up for the marrow-fat which is contained in them. Their sinews are used for strings and backs for their bows, for thread to string their beads and sew their dresses. The feet of the animal are boiled with their hoofs for the glue they contain, for fastening their arrow points, and many other uses. The hair from the head and shoulder, which is long, is twisted and braided into halters, and the tail is used for a fly brush.[11]

Thus, the nomadic Sioux moved their campsites frequently to follow the vital herds of buffalo across the plains. For the Oglala Sioux of young Curly's tribe, the buffalo hunt was a major event. The Indian warrior was usually armed with a short bow, to use when shooting from astride a galloping buffalo pony. These alert and intelligent horses were trained to follow game and press close to the side of running buffalo while the Indian rider exerted guidance by the pressure of his knees. Arrows were carefully crafted and selected, with sharpened tips of bone, flint, or steel. The arrows used in the buffalo hunt were usually barbed and held fast to the shaft. However, the arrows used by the Sioux in combat often had loosely attached barbs that would come off when the shaft was detached, leaving the barb in the wound. The arrows were carried in a quiver slung over the shoulder. As Walter Prescott Webb writes, "The Plains Indian was a formidable warrior in his country . . . he could carry a hundred arrows, and . . . he could shoot them from his running horse so rapidly as to keep one or more in the air all the time and with such force as to drive the shaft entirely through the body of the buffalo."[12]

Although the buffalo was a vital part of the Teton Sioux economy, there was other tribal commerce on the Great Plains. White traders supplied pots, pans, guns, knives, and even decorative ornaments such as beads, in return for animal furs and skins. These items and even sugar and coffee could soon be found in the Sioux camps. Some scholars believe that the Sioux became dependent on whites for material goods. Edward Lazarus writes, "The introduction of firearms, cooking utensils, and a host of other items had drastically reduced the workload of their [Sioux] hunting culture and the tools of western civilization were becoming everyday necessities of Sioux life."[13]

The first recorded contact between the Teton and the new nation, the United States, occurred in late August 1804 when the expedition of Meriwether Lewis and William Clark reached Teton territory. Lewis and Clark had been sent by President Thomas Jefferson's administration to explore the vast territory the United States had purchased from France in 1803, under the terms of the Louisiana Purchase.

At first, the Sioux had no concept of landowning and the Americans were not treated very well. After delighting their visitors with feasting, dancing, and even smoking the sacred pipe, the Sioux pretended to be dissatisfied with the gifts offered by the explorers. Things got tense as the Sioux threatened to detain two officers. But the difficulty was resolved in a council meeting with Chief Black Buffalo. The Americans were welcomed peacefully; they distributed government medals to the Indians and conferred American citizenship on a Sioux baby. However, the Sioux reacted to white Americans with their own logic. How could a president (Jefferson) buy land from an emperor (Napoleon) when neither man had ever seen it or even set foot on it? To the Sioux, who saw land as belonging to the people living on it and from it, it made little sense.

The Lewis and Clark expedition had opened the

upper Missouri territory to United States trade and commerce. Whether the Sioux knew it or not, that contact marked the beginning of the end for their way of life on the Plains. White Americans soon began to compete with the British by founding the Missouri and American fur companies in 1808. After the War of 1812, English traders gradually withdrew and American trading companies soon had a monopoly on the fur trade throughout the upper Missouri region where the Sioux lived.[14]

As American interest in the Sioux region grew, a steady trickle of trappers, traders, mountain men and women, and soldiers flowed onto the Plains. But the land was abundant, game was plentiful and, for the Sioux, life remained much as it had always been—pleasing and good.

In 1825 the United States government organized the Yellowstone Expedition led by General Henry Atkinson and Major Benjamin O'Fallon. This second official foray into Sioux territory was to show the Indians along the Upper Missouri the power of American military strength. Atkinson and O'Fallon led 475 men into Teton country in late June and early July, concluding three separate treaties with the Sioux. Those treaties emphasized American supremacy over Sioux territory, reserved the right to regulate commerce with the Sioux tribes and, at the same time, limited the Indians to trading privileges only with United States citizens. The Sioux had to agree to apprehend foreign traders and all criminals, Indian or white, for prosecution by American authorities. In return, the United States pledged to protect the Sioux and their property and to prosecute anyone who violated the law. The United States agreed to "receive [the Sioux] into their friendship" and to give to the Sioux "such benefits and acts of kindness as may be convenient" to the president.

On Independence Day, 1825, the Americans sealed their bargain with the Tetons, whose tribe had tripled in size to 10,000 since the Lewis and Clark expedition. A young American officer, Lieutenant William Harney, read the Declaration of Independence to the gathered Sioux. The

21

Americans dazzled the Indians with a display of fireworks that lit up the night sky. And so the Indians sat peacefully along the banks of a river as they listened to Thomas Jefferson's inspiring words about the rights of human beings, the obligation of government, and the pursuit of happiness. As one historian observed, "How incomprehensible the idea of sovereignty must have seemed to a people who knew nothing of kings or nation-states; how foreign the idea of trade regulation to a people who never coined money, who wrote no laws."[15]

Increased contact and trade with the whites after 1825 brought the Sioux a measure of prosperity, with many new gadgets and weapons that enhanced Sioux life on the Plains. However, there was a heavy price. Along with their goods, the whites unwittingly brought the Indians new diseases like cholera, smallpox, and venereal disease. Worst of all they brought the Indians alcohol. The Plains Indians craved the whites' brew but they had little tolerance of it. The Sioux called alcohol *mini wakan*, or "the water that makes men foolish." After the introduction of alcohol into their camps, violence among the Sioux increased dramatically. But the American government did practically nothing to stop the traders from passing whiskey to the Indians; after all, it was part of the increasingly lucrative profits of the fur trade.[16]

As alcohol became common currency on the plains, Americans were getting richer and Indians were getting drunk and impoverished. To many Americans in the government during these years, it wasn't a very troubling issue. If the Plains Indians ever became too violent there was always the army.

Among the Americans who traveled westward to the plains to live among the Sioux in these relatively tranquil years was Francis Parkman. Parkman, a son of proper Boston society and a graduate of Harvard University, went to live among the Sioux in 1846 when he was twenty-three years of age. One historian believes that young Crazy Horse (Curly), who was around five years old at the time, may have been among the band that Parkman visited that summer.[17]

Parkman had been a devoted reader of the novels of James Fenimore Cooper. Like Cooper, he viewed the Indian romantically, "as noble savage" living heroically in the primitive American wilderness. However, once Parkman actually lived with the Sioux, his point of view underwent subtle but important changes and he rejected Cooper's simpler view of Indian life. Parkman came to understand that Cooper's Indians were not very real. They "are for the most part either superficially or falsely drawn; while the long conversations which he puts into their mouths, are as truthless as they are tiresome."[18]

The more Parkman observed the Sioux, the more he believed that the Indian way of life would never be compatible with that of whites. While Parkman admired Sioux courage in the hunt and on the battlefield, he saw the Sioux as warlike and in some respects like quarrelsome children. Parkman admired the family bonds that kept the Oglalas together, but was critical of the way children were raised and the seeming lack of discipline in Sioux households. He observed the Sioux

> like most other Indians were very fond of their children, whom they indulged to excess, and never punished, except in extreme cases. . . . Their offspring became sufficiently undutiful and disobedient under this system of education, which tends not a little to foster that wild idea of liberty and utter intolerance of restraint which lie at the foundation of the Indian character.[19]

Parkman was shocked by the Oglalas' "laziness and obscenity" and horrified by "their manners, dress and smell."[20]

Living among the Oglala Sioux, Parkman participated in their buffalo hunts and moved with them as the nomadic tribe traversed the Great Plains to follow the herds. In many ways Francis Parkman was one of the first modern journalists—he wrote down what he observed and felt and then sent it back for consumption by the American people. Parkman was basically an historian but also wanted to participate in the history that he observed and wrote about. Thus, in his classic book, *The Oregon Trail,* Parkman created for his Eastern readers a powerful view of the adventure of everyday Indian life in a Sioux village on the Plains.

Parkman was guided on his journey by Henry Chattilon, an illiterate hunter married to an Oglala woman. They were greeted at Horse Creek by the Oglala chief, Old Smoke, and his "favorite squaw," who escorted them into the Sioux village. Parkman painted a vivid picture of young Crazy Horse's world:

> *Warriors, women and children swarmed like bees; hundreds of dogs, of all sizes and colors, ran restlessly about; and close at hand, the wide shallow stream was alive with boys, girls and young squaws, splashing, screaming, and laughing in the water. At the same time a long train of emigrants with their heavy wagons was crossing the creek, and dragging on in slow procession by the encampment of the people who they and their descendants, in the space of a century, are to sweep from the face of the earth.*[21]

Parkman's observations would have led readers to believe that all was relatively well between the Indians and the new arrivals on the Plains, as a steady flow of white pioneers in wagon trains crossed into Indian territory. But the Sioux had reasons for allowing the whites to pass without incident, and beneath the tranquil surface, tension was mounting. Parkman noted that it was customary for the Indians to enter the camps of westward-bound settlers, demanding "a feast" as part of the price for peaceful passage through their territory. Actually, the "feast" was little more than a few biscuits and a cup of coffee. With increasing contact with the whites, the Sioux had come to crave coffee almost as much as alcohol. Parkman recorded growing ill feelings, even in the 1840s, between the Sioux and the settlers arriving at Fort Laramie, an outpost established by the American Fur Company. Parkman wrote,

> With each emigrant party that arrived at Fort Laramie . . . the Indians grew more rapacious and presumptuous. . . . . They began to openly threaten the emigrants with destruction and actually fired upon one or two parties of them. A military force and military law are urgently called for in that perilous region; and unless troops are speedily stationed at Fort Laramie, or elsewhere in the neighborhood, both emigrants and other travelers will be exposed to most imminent risks.[22]

Parkman knew that the United States government held little sway with the Indians on the Plains in the 1840s, since the closest American troops were seven hundred miles to the east. He predicted trouble ahead between the Sioux and the settlers streaming west along the Oregon Trail:

> The Ogillallah [sic], the Brulé, and the other western bands of the Dahcotah or Sioux are thorough savages, unchanged by any contact with civilization. Not one of them can speak a European tongue, or has ever visited an American settlement. Until within a year or two, when the emigrants began to pass through their country on the way to Oregon, they had seen no whites, except the few employed about the Fur Company's posts. They thought them a wise people, inferior only to themselves, living in leather lodges, like their own, and subsisting on buffalo. But when the swarm of Memeaska [the Indian name for the whites], with their oxen and wagons, began to invade them, their astonishment was unbounded. They could scarcely believe that the earth contained such a multitude of white men. Their wonder is now giving way to indignation; and the result, unless vigilantly guarded against, may be lamentable in the extreme.[23]

During his years spent with the Indians on the Great Plains, George Caitlin painted this scene of an Indian tribe on the move.

The Sioux warrior seemed happiest riding his pony across the wide prairie. Parkman noticed that the Oglala Sioux were always on the move. During the good weather they sometimes picked up and moved their villages once or twice a week, although in winter moves were less frequent. The speed with which a village could be disassembled and made ready for travel was remarkable. Their tipis or lodges could be taken down and put back up in less than an hour. In a few hours an entire village could be packed up and gone.[24]

On one occasion Parkman awoke one morning to find the entire Oglala village in an uproar. Apparently, the Indians had decided to move during the night. Their cone-shaped lodges had been reduced to nothing but skeletons of poles as the women yanked off the leather coverings

26

from the lodges, lashed them to shaggy packhorses, and packed the gear.

The entire village disappeared in a matter of minutes. The scene appeared chaotic as the squaws bustled about their work and the old women shrieked at one another. But everyone knew and did their tasks, while the warriors sat, unconcerned, around their dwindling campfires. Parkman wrote,

> The sun never shone upon a more strange array. Here were the heavy-laden packhorses, some wretched old women leading them, and two or three children clinging to their backs. Here were mules or ponies covered from head to tail with gaudy trappings and mounted by some gay young squaw, grinning bashfulness and pleasures.... Boys with miniature bows and arrows wandered over the plains, little naked children ran along on foot, and numberless dogs scampered among the feet of the horses. The young braves, gaudy with paint and feathers, rode in groups, often galloping, two or three at once along the line, to try the speed of their horses.[25]

As part of the Oglala encampment that summer Parkman participated in a ritual buffalo hunt, observing the skilled Sioux warriors scattering the huge animals while riding at breakneck speed into the center of a great herd.

> Looking up, I saw a whole body of Indians ... each hunter, as if by a common impulse, violently struck his horse, each horse sprang forward, and, scattering in the charge in order to assail the entire herd at once, we all rushed headlong upon the buffalo.... The dust cleared away and the buffalo could be seen scattering ... flying over the plain singly, or in long files and small compact bodies, while behind them followed the Indians, riding at furious speed, and yelling as they launched arrow after arrow into their sides. The carcasses were strewn thickly over the ground. Here and there stood wounded buffalo, their bleeding sides feathered with arrows....[26]

Parkman also had quiet moments with his new friends. He often joined his Oglala hosts for an evening of smoking and storytelling. As in many tribes, the elders were the repository of tribal history, tradition, and legends. One night his old Oglala friend Mene-Sela gave out a few fragments of an ancient Sioux tale but withheld most of the story out of superstition and to keep Parkman with the tribe through the next winter. As the old Sioux told Parkman, "It is a bad thing to tell the tales in summer. Stay with us till next winter and I will tell you everything I know; but now our war parties are going out, and our young men will be killed if I sit down to tell stories before the frost begins."[27]

On the whole, Parkman liked and admired the Sioux. He found them gracious hosts, brave, honest, and generous. He saw that the Oglalas took care of themselves, saw to their children, honored their elders, and were a contented and happy people. Parkman described occasions when he saw the Sioux "give away the whole of their possessions and reduce themselves to nakedness and want." One time Parkman observed a Sioux warrior lead his two best horses into the center of the village whereupon he generously presented them to his friends.[28]

Parkman found that life was good for the Oglala Sioux on the Great Plains. The old warrior ways and the self-sufficient lifestyle had changed very little. Buffalo and other game were still plentiful, and trade with the advancing white settlers brought the Indians whiskey, coffee, sugar, metal, and guns they wanted. But contact between the Indian and the white world would ultimately produce problems.[29]

Some of the younger Sioux understood that their people had arrived at a crossroads in their relations with the whites. Sitting Bull, a Hunkpapa Sioux leader born around 1831, urged that the tribe leave the Oregon Trail region where they lived and hunted, give up their dependence on white traders and their goods, and return to the ways of their ancestors. Sitting Bull said, "The whites may get me at last, but I will still have good times till then. You are fools to make yourselves slaves to a piece of fat bacon, some hard-tack, and a little sugar and coffee."[30]

Except for a few isolated skirmishes between Indians and whites, the 1840s on the Great Plains were peaceful. If traders, hunters, or settlers carelessly exposed themselves, they risked losing not only their possessions but their lives. But many Sioux tribes and bands remained as ignorant of the encroaching American society by 1850 as they had been when Lewis and Clark first made contact at the beginning of the century.

Most Americans had not envisioned expansion west beyond the Mississippi River. But by the 1840s many Americans were caught up in the concept of Manifest Destiny—that the United States would ultimately stretch all the way to the Pacific Ocean. Thus, with a burgeoning population of 23.2 million people and a land mass that by the end of the Mexican War extended to some 3 million square miles, the Americans would not allow a few thousand Plains Indians to stand in the path of American destiny, progress, and civilization.[31]

The Indians would either take up the way of the white settlers, or step aside, or be pushed out of the way. In 1842 —the year Crazy Horse was born—eighteen pioneer wagons crossed into Sioux territory, opening the attack on the Plains Indians' way of life. The settlers, bound for Oregon, had started in Independence, Missouri, and had moved steadily northwest to the Platte River and on for hundreds of miles following the Platte until they crossed Kansas, Nebraska, and Wyoming—penetrating the heart of the lands that had been the vital buffalo hunting grounds of the Teton Sioux for generations.[32] No matter how hard the Sioux may have attempted to accept the intrusion of the whites, and no matter what policies of war or peace their leaders put into practice, there seemed an incompatibility between Indian and white that would inevitably lead to conflict and catastrophe. Reflecting the attitudes of his time, Francis Parkman wrote:

For the most part, a civilized white man can discover very few points of sympathy between his own nature and that of an Indian. With every disposition to do justice to their good qualities, he must be conscious that an impassable gulf lies between him and his red brethren. Nay, so alien to himself do they appear, that, after breathing the air of the prairie for a few months or weeks, he begins to look upon them as a troublesome and dangerous species of wild beast.[33]

It must be remembered that Parkman liked the Indians. However, with friends like Parkman, the Sioux Nation didn't need any enemies.

CHAPTER TWO

BECOMING A WARRIOR

In the two decades before the Civil War, the American people were preoccupied with one issue: slavery. Everyone had an opinion, and as Thomas Jefferson observed as early as 1820, the issue of slavery was like "a firebell in the night" that threatened to one day destroy the nation.

By the 1830s sections were in clear disagreement. The abolitionist movement had grown from a tiny group of uncompromising stalwarts demanding an immediate end to the "peculiar institution" of slavery, and the country was torn by the issue. The split between North and South became the major political issue, with the industrial, non-slaveholding North a distinct entity from the the King Cotton economy of the agricultural, slave South.

In the 1840s, the nation's churches entered the dispute. Northern religious leaders were generally opposed to slavery, while southern religious leaders, often citing the Bible, supported it. In the 1850s the political parties split. The new Republican party, formed in 1854, opposed slavery and its expansion; Democrats generally supported slavery where it existed. And in a further split, the southern Democrats supported slavery's expansion into the territories.

And finally, in 1860, with the election of the Republican party's antislavery candidate, Abraham Lincoln, to the

Army forts were lonely outposts surrounded on all sides by the vast stretches of the Great Plains.

presidency, the nation itself split. The tragic Civil War that ensued (1861–1865) cost over 600,000 American lives, much of the national treasury, the life of a great leader—Lincoln was the first United States president to be assassinated—and, in one way or another, touched the life of every American.

With white Americans preoccupied with slavery between 1840 and 1860, little attention was given to the question of the Native Americans who still roamed freely west of the Mississippi River. Thus, in the years that the young Oglala boy Curly was coming of age, Sioux life on the Plains remained unchanged. The upper country along the Shell River was as far as the whites had come. As Mari Sandoz wrote, "the gleaming 'dobe walls and bastions of Fort Laramie, the soldier town . . . was only a little island of whites in a great sea of Indian country two thousand miles wide."[1]

Curly grew up in an Indian family typical of Oglala tribal life. His father, Crazy Horse, was not a warrior but was known around the Oglala village as a mystic—a man who possessed healing powers and was an interpreter of dreams. He had two wives, both sisters of the well-known

32

Brulé warrior Spotted Tail. When Curly's birth mother died, his father's other wife became Curly's second mother. It was customary for Sioux men to have more than one wife, and often the men married sisters in the belief that two women who were related and had lived in the same household would get along better.[2]

Growing up, Curly was instilled with a sense of self-worth and pride in belonging to the distinct tribal entity called the Oglala Sioux. The Sioux, as Francis Parkman observed, treated their children with great love and affection. Mothers nursed communally and fathers sometimes played with their children for hours. After spending his infancy on a cradleboard, Curly was free to roam his village. Like most Sioux children he knew no restraints and was never struck in anger by his parents or any adult.[3]

There was no formal schooling for children in Sioux tribal society. Children generally learned by watching adults or other children. Whether it was early toilet training or the simple children's games, Curly learned by watching others as he grew to understand and gain knowledge of the customs of his tribe. He scampered around the Oglala campsites naked during the warm springs and hot summers until he was seven or eight. Even in the cold winters of the Great Plains, clothes were seldom a necessity for an Indian youngster crawling around the floor near the warmth of the campfire in his family tipi.

As Curly approached adolescence, he put away the toy tipis and carved implements of childhood for rougher games of skill. These games were challenging and prepared the Indian boys for their tasks as family providers and Oglala warriors. The games emphasized strength, speed, agility, endurance, skill with weapons, and the ability to withstand pain. The young Sioux boys played "Throw at Each Other with Mud," attacking one another with mud balls mounted on and hurled from sticks; or they played "Buffalo Hunt," where they aimed their bows and arrows at a simulated buffalo heart cut from a cactus plant. If a shooter missed, the boy holding the buffalo's heart chased him, trying to poke him in the rear with the spikes of the prickly prairie plant.[4]

In adolescence, Curly killed his first buffalo and rode his first wild horse. As a result of his accomplishments he was permitted to take a new name, His Horse Looking. Although his father called him by his new name, as did his close friend High Back Bone (named Hump for short), the women and most of the young men in the tribe still saw him as a youngster and called him Curly.

It was customary for Sioux teenage boys to pair off with special partners called *kolas*. The boys shared friendship and knowledge and, eventually, hunted and fought the Oglala's enemies together. Many Oglalas were surprised that Hump, who was older than Curly, chose the sandy-haired youngster as his *kola*. Young Hump, already known as a Minniconjou-Oglala warrior, could have chosen the son of a great Oglala fighting man as his protégé, or younger Indian brother. That Hump chose Curly, "this strange boy of the light skin, the hair of yellow and soft as a prairie chicken's," was something of an honor for Curly because Hump was on his way to joining the Sioux warrior society, "the Akicita."[5]

The Akicita provided what little law enforcement was needed in Sioux tribal society. The Sioux loved freedom and hated any form of restraint. Still, they were a disciplined people. Each band had its own chief, but the chief did not have absolute authority over the people's lives. The chief's duty was to carry out the will of the majority and to safeguard the band's tribal customs, traditions, and religion. The chief could influence decision making but could rarely issue a decree or law without taking into account the wishes of the tribe. A man could become a chief through bravery in war, through wealth, or he might even inherit the rank from his father. But the Sioux understood the corruptive influence of too much power, and no single chief was permitted to rule the entire Sioux tribe.[6]

Major decisions within the overall tribe were usually left to the tribal council that met when the various Sioux bands came together in the summer months. The tribal council governed the Sioux through deputies who enforced the rules with tribal soldiers. Among the Oglala Sioux, the tribal council consisted of chiefs from seven bands who were chosen by the elder men of the tribe. These chiefs then chose deputies, "Shirt-Wearers," who wore shirts fringed with animal hair as a badge of office. They, in turn, exercised their authority and that of the tribal council through tribal soldiers chosen from the society known as the Akicita. These tribal police commanded respect and obedience. The Akicita saw that there was general order when the camp moved, oversaw the buffalo hunt, and had an additional function: if a Sioux warrior committed murder, the Akicita were called upon to render swift and merciless tribal justice. As the Oglalas told one writer, the Akicita "see that no one kills another, but in case one does, they either kill him or destroy all his property, kill his horses, destroy his tipi . . . ."[7]

Francis Parkman observed that the Akicita were among

> the most important executive functionaries in an Indian village. The office is one of considerable honor, being confided only to men of courage and repute. . . . While very few Ogillallah [sic] chiefs could venture without risk of their lives to strike or lay hands upon the meanest of their people, the "soldiers," in the discharge of their appropriate functions, have full license to make use of these and similar acts of coercion.[8]

Oglala young men with ambitions to join the Akicita first had to master hunting and fighting. This meant that the harsh prairie had to be challenged and overcome. As a result of his father's efforts and his friendship with Hump, Curly was a skilled hunter by the time he was a teenager. Curly's father, Crazy Horse, taught him the various species of birds and the meaning of their different calls. Crazy Horse wanted his son to know how to find water, and to know which side of the trees had light-colored bark to determine directions, and the medicinal value of countless plants and shrubs.

His father encouraged Curly to pay attention and learn from the many animals of the vast prairie. Watching birds of prey like the hawk and the eagle, Curly understood the importance of patience to the hunter; from the wolf and coyote, Curly learned how to evade capture; from the herds of wild horses, he learned how to find water. Curly saw that when a herd of wild horses moved steadily across the plains they were heading for water and, if the herd was scattered and grazing peacefully, that they had come from water. By the time he was ten or eleven Curly was able to read tracks and animal droppings the way a white youngster could read a primer.[9]

Like every Sioux boy Curly waited for the day when he could join the warriors of his village on a war party or on a raid to steal horses from an enemy tribe. For the Oglala, Parkman observed, "War is the breath of their nostrils. Against most of the neighboring tribes they cherish a rancorous hatred, transmitted from father to son, and inflamed by constant aggression and retaliation. Many times a year, in every village, the Great Spirit is called upon, fasts are made, the war parade is celebrated, and the warriors go out by handfuls at a time against the enemy."[10]

The Sioux warriors set out wearing crests of eagle feathers, colorful robes, and the scalp locks of their enemies hanging from the fringes of their buckskin jackets. They carried painted shields decorated with feathers and a few wore large feathered warbonnets signifying leadership and bravery. Every warrior carried a bow and arrows and even their buffalo ponies were painted with designs for war. Francis Parkman described an Oglala war party in *The Oregon Trail*:

> Savage figures, with quivers at their backs, and guns, lances, or tomahawks in their hands, sat on horseback, motionless as statues, their arms crossed on their

36

*breasts and their eyes fixed in a steady unwavering
gaze. . . . Others stood erect, wrapped from head to foot
in their long white robes of buffalo hide.*[11]

A returning Sioux war party was even more impressive:

*The warriors rode three times round the village; and as
each noted champion passed, the old women would
scream out his name, to honor his bravery and excite the
emulation of the younger warriors. Little urchins, not two
years old, followed the warlike pageant with glittering
eyes, and gazed with eager admiration at the heroes of
the tribe.*[12]

One historian suggests that Curly, an independent and
ambitious young Oglala, probably sneaked off at the age of
eleven or twelve to join the fighting men of his village in a
raid. But any young Sioux had to prove that he was worthy
to become a warrior. Thus, younger members of an Oglala
raiding party were usually kept in the background, watching the horses.[13]

During the 1840s, an increasing number of whites
began streaming into Sioux territory. The Oglalas of Curly's
band were divided on how to deal with them. Bull Bear, a
powerful chief who headed an Oglala band called Koya,
made it difficult for the whites. Old Smoke, chief of Curly's
band, the Bad Faces, enjoyed the wide variety of goods that
the white traders offered. The early skirmishes between the
Oglalas and the whites were mostly minor, but the issues
dividing the Sioux over how they would deal with the
whites were complex. While the immediate conflicts arose
over the precious material goods the Sioux wanted, and
ultimately demanded, as a price for an uneasy peace, the
real situation involved a dramatic clash of cultures.

During Curly's boyhood, a number of developments
had marked effects on him. In the summer of 1845 the first
U.S. soldiers marched up the Platte River under Colonel
Stephen W. Kearny. The white settlers were disturbed that

some younger Sioux warriors were raiding the western-bound wagon trains along the Oregon Trail, and stealing stray cattle and horses. To the settlers, the Indians were lazy robbers, guilty of extortion. One day the younger Sioux braves would raid the wagon trains; the next day they would show up at Fort Laramie to beg for coffee and sugar. But the Sioux didn't understand. If they "found" a cow or horse wandering on the wide-open prairie, did the animal not belong to them? That had always been the custom. The Sioux felt that the whites had far more than they needed and were being stingy and greedy.

Colonel Kearny met with the Oglalas from Old Smoke's band as well as with other Oglalas who camped on the Laramie River. He warned the Sioux that if they went on harassing the passing settlers they would be dealt with harshly. But the Oglalas continued their attacks.[14]

A second influence began to appear in 1849 and took a heavy toll on all the tribes across the Great Plains: epidemics of the white settlers' diseases of cholera, measles, and smallpox. The Cheyenne and Sioux were decimated by these diseases. At first, the Indians tried to flee. The Sioux moved north and the Cheyenne fled in every direction. The Brulés and Oglalas moved back to their old campsites along the White River in South Dakota. One camp they entered was lifeless—filled with dead people. By the end of a year cholera had wiped out nearly half of the Cheyenne, the Pawnee, and many Sioux. In 1850 cholera was followed by smallpox. Again, hundreds of Indians died. The Indians grumbled that these diseases were brought to the plains by the whites using some form of wicked magic. Some Sioux and Cheyenne even began speaking of vengeance against the whites.[15]

Magic, of course, played no role in the plagues. With the discovery of gold in California in 1848, what had been a trickle of emigrants flowing west for most of the 1840s became a torrent. The Mormon settlers had crossed the Sioux lands in 1847. Then, the gold rush drew 90,000 settlers west by way of the Oregon Trail. As one scholar noted,

"All that had gone before was nothing compared to the unending lines of wagons that moved across the plains from horizon to horizon during the traveling months of late spring and early summer."[16] The emigrants brought everything they owned in their cloth-covered wagons, appearing like billowing clouds along the Oregon Trail, making their way into the ancestral homeland of the Sioux and the other Plains tribes. Their unseen baggage included a disregard for the prairie and a host of diseases against which the Indians had no immunity.

These "forty-niners" trampled the summer grazing range—the grasslands that had fed some 15 million buffalo. The stream of eager settlers tore up the countryside, and fouled the land. They littered the trails with refuse, leaving behind discarded tools, clothing, wagon parts, rotting food, and even carcasses of dead animals. The smell of rotting garbage and decaying carcasses forced away the buffalo. They divided into northern and southern herds, and never returned in sufficient numbers for hunting.[17]

As Edward Lazarus observed, the emigrant movement had far-reaching repercussions for the Sioux.

> The Oregon Trail did more than move the buffalo; it destroyed the hunting pattern of the Sioux, forcing them to follow the herds to the fringes of their domain and expose themselves to the raids of their enemies. The Teton had no trouble attributing blame for their predicament, but they grew frustrated, arguing among themselves about what to do with the white intruders. The Sioux threatened; they robbed; they shot up caravans; but they could not stop the emigrants.[18]

By 1851 the epidemics had waned but the whites, aware of continuing unrest among the Indians, tried to ward off new trouble by inviting all the tribes living near or along the Platte River to attend a council at Fort Laramie, which the United States government had purchased from the American Fur Company in 1849. A few hundred troops were stationed at the fort to protect the Oregon Trail; but this symbolic force hardly threatened the Indians. Fort Laramie was only a plains outpost, surrounded by thousands of potentially hostile Indians.[19]

There was precedent for a large-scale meeting with the Sioux and other tribes. The American government wanted a treaty granting settlers unobstructed passage on the Oregon Trail. In July 1851, the eastern Sioux signed away all their valuable lands in Iowa and Minnesota, except for a twenty-mile-wide reservation along the Minnesota River. The Indians were to be paid $68,000 a year for fifty years. However, they got practically nothing, for much of the purchase money was applied to a $210,000 "debt" and stolen from the Sioux by unscrupulous traders.[20]

Realizing that they could never guard the trails through Indian country with the small contingent of soldiers at Fort Laramie, the United States government attempted to negotiate a settlement with the Plains Indians. In 1850 Congress appropriated $100,000 "for holding treaties with the wild tribes of the prairies," and the Commissioner of Indian Affairs in Washington gave his agents instructions to make arrangements for a grand council at Fort Laramie in September 1851.[21]

Between eight and twelve thousand Indians flocked to Fort Laramie from every corner of the Great Plains. They arrived with all their goods, their dogs, and their horses, and pitched their camps. In addition to the various bands of Sioux, there were Cheyenne, Crow, Mandan, Arikara, Shoshone—tribes that had been enemies were gathering for the largest meeting of Plains Indians that had ever taken place.[22]

Curly, in his tenth year, was in the throng. For the first time he met youngsters from tribes who were enemies of the Oglalas. The Indian boys raced ponies and played games while the white agents and Indian leaders met in a large tent. The boys used sign language, the form of communication on the plains where each tribe spoke a different language. There were great feasts as the Laramie meeting lasted almost a month, concluding with the Indians signing the treaty and receiving the government's gifts.[23]

But the Laramie Treaty of 1851 was only a stopgap. It appeared to resolve the immediate problem of the Indians' raids on the settlers along the Oregon Trail, but it disregarded the Indian way of life and the Plains culture.

Many of the Indian leaders, aware that the summer buffalo hunts had been disastrous, and facing the approach of winter, wanted peace with the whites. They also wanted white goods. Thus, they recognized the whites' right to use the Oregon Trail, or the "Holy Road" as the Indians called it. They gave the United States the right to construct roads and build military outposts within their territory. In addition, the Indians promised to make restitution for all Indian crimes against the settlers committed after signing the treaty. This clause ultimately caused great trouble and misunderstanding. To whites, all Indians were alike. If the Hunkpapa Sioux attacked, it was the same as if the Oglala Sioux had violated the treaty. Indian tribal governance was far different from the government in Washington, D.C.; but on the prairie, no attempt was ever made to differentiate between the guilty and the innocent on either side.

In return for their concessions, the Laramie Treaty provided the Plains Indians with what appeared to be an acceptable deal. The United States agreed to protect the Indians from marauding settlers and frontiersmen. The government also agreed to pay the tribes a total of $50,000 a year for the next fifty years. And, for the first time, the American government formally recognized what Chief Justice John Marshall had written in 1830—that the Indian tribes were "distinct, independent, political communities."

In other clauses, the treaty outlawed many aspects of the Plains Indian way of life: war parties, raids, and stealing horses—all activities that were looked upon as honorable by the Indians and that often elevated warriors to leadership status were forbidden. Land matters were even more complicated. Although the agreement recognized that the Sioux owned over sixty million acres of land from the

Missouri River in the east to beyond the Black Hills in the Dakotas, and from the Platte River to the Heart River in the north, the Powder River country, which had belonged to the Sioux since 1822, was returned to the hated Crow tribe, and the land south of the Platte River was given to the Kiowa. This ensured that the Indians would once again be warring with one another. Soon Sioux war parties were indeed raiding Crow villages near the Big Horn mountains. To make matters worse, the United States Senate immediately broke the terms of the treaty. Instead of payments for fifty years, the Senate voted to reduce the term to ten years with five additional years added only at the discretion of the president. Historian Edward Lazarus wrote, "The Sioux had no idea that the United States had amended the treaty unilaterally. . . . The Laramie Treaty failed even before it became law. One party had revised its terms; the other party ignored them."[24]

Another indication of the arrogance of the United States officials and of white ignorance of the Indians' way of life was the American government's insistence that each of the Plains tribes have a single chief. Instead of the Oglala Chief Old Smoke, who had always been friendly to the whites, the Americans selected the Brulé Sioux chief, Conquering Bear. When Conquering Bear was permitted to distribute the whites' gifts to the tribes, he gained status. The goods arrived every year and the whites dealt with the Indians only through the chiefs they had chosen. Thus, the American government undermined Sioux tribal structure, which had always avoided concentrating power in the hands of a single leader.[25]

Not every Sioux chief signed the Fort Laramie agreement, and there was much intertribal disagreement. The Hunkpapas and Blackfeet couldn't accept ending their warfare with their hereditary enemies, the Crows, the Arikaras, and the Assiniboines. But Sitting Bull's Hunkpapas were more unified in their opposition to the treaty than the Minniconjous, Sans Arcs, and Two Kettles. However, there was even disagreement among the Hunkpapas and

Blackfeet. As historian Robert M. Utley observed, "The issue pitted band against band. . . . More vehemently, it pitted youth against age. Older men dreamed of peace and did not object strenuously to taking the white man's presents. Young men had no patience with peace talk. War offered the only path to honor, status, and rank. . . ."[26]

Nevertheless, Old Smoke's Oglalas left the great council at Fort Laramie in a happy frame of mind. Young Curly and his band headed north to hunt buffalo before settling in for the winter of 1851–52. By spring, Old Smoke's Oglalas returned to the Fort Laramie area and immediately violated the treaty by harassing the passing wagon trains. At the same time, they waited for the coveted goods promised to them by the treaty.

Curly was now approaching the age of a warrior and very likely took part in these raids. He had become a quiet, reserved young man. He had grown to nearly six feet, he was thin, and his hair and complexion had remained very light. Short Bull, a brave who grew up with Curly, recalled that "his features were not like those of the rest of us. His face was not broad, and he had a sharp, high nose. He had black eyes that hardly ever looked straight at a man, but they didn't miss much that was going on all the same." Curly also acted different. Unlike many boastful young men of his tribe, Curly was very modest and did not brag about his exploits or prowess. As Curly's friend He Dog remembered, "He never spoke in council and attended very few. There was no special reason for this, it was just his nature. He was a very quiet man except when there was fighting." Also, unlike many other braves, Curly refused initiation into Sioux warrior society by not participating in the Sioux custom called the Sun Dance. In that ritual, young men suspended themselves from a pole by ropes ending in sharp-pointed skewers that pierced the muscles of their chests. The dancers offered themselves up to the Great Spirit by tearing the skin of their chests and undergoing excruciating pain. Sioux men wore the scars of the Sun Dance as a badge of great honor, but not Curly. It was not

that he wanted to avoid pain or was afraid. He felt no need to take part in the painful ceremony. He had made up his mind to become an Oglala warrior and to make his mark in his tribe in his own way.[27]

As he grew into his teens, Curly became increasingly aware of the growing friction between his people and the whites. Like many Sioux, he didn't understand how the whites could expect the Indian to honor a treaty that declared that only the head chief could arrest a person who initiated trouble between the Indians and the whites. Why didn't the whites understand the Sioux? It was the custom of his people for chiefs to lead the councils of the war parties. But chiefs were never responsible for anything individual warriors did, and they were certainly not in charge of disciplining Oglalas who broke the law. And Curly also wondered who would punish the whites if they broke the treaty by shooting an Indian.

It seemed an old tribal argument: what to do about the white settlers? The older chiefs wanted peace. The Fort Laramie Treaty showed this. But what would happen if one day the younger men turned away from peace? Curly had seen the white soldiers at the fort take away their own people in chains. His friend Hump said that it was better to die fighting the whites than to allow them to take you away in chains.

For an intelligent young Oglala man approaching adulthood, these were troubling issues. Were the whites to be trusted? Why should the Sioux stop raiding the settlers who were driving away the buffalo and destroying the very face of the land. In the spring of 1852 Curly, son of Crazy Horse, pondered these questions that would soon become critical as the plains were lit by the fires of conflict.[28]

Initiation into the Sioux warrior class
was marked by the painful Sun Dance.

CHAPTER THREE

CURLY'S FIRST BATTLE

One key factor in the defeat of the native tribes in North America was their consistent failure to unite. Perhaps the only way the Native Americans could have protected their independence and way of life would have been for them to suppress a major aspect of their culture—their incessant tribal warfare—and unite against their common and dangerous foe. But tribal customs and differences were too great. The whites benefited from the Indians' inability to join forces and their continued dependence on the cherished goods the whites provided.

Until the nineteenth century, Tecumseh was the one Indian leader who understood that the American Indian way of life was doomed if the tribes failed to unite against the whites. Tecumseh was a great Shawnee warrior. The Shawnee were an agricultural people who lived in what could be called towns in the regions that are today the states of Ohio, Kentucky, and Indiana.

Tecumseh viewed the settlers' advance on the early western frontier of Ohio and Kentucky as a threat to his people. After the American Revolution he allied himself with the British, who were attempting to recapture their lost colonies. At one point Tecumseh and his brother, the Prophet, journeyed through the Northeast to the frontier in an attempt to unite the various tribes. Tecumseh was usually welcomed by the Delawares, Senecas, Oneidas, Ononda, Mohawks, Tuscarawas, and many other tribes, who often gathered to listen to this stranger who preached a message of Indian unification that they never heard before.

In the summer of 1803 Tecumseh traveled far up the Mississippi to visit the Dakotas, a subtribe of the Sioux, and the bands that made up the Santee division of the mighty Sioux nation. Tecumseh's message was simple: the whites could not be trusted. Their promises were as hollow as their treaties. If the Sioux were not willing to unite as "red brothers," all Indians, not only the Sioux, would be defeated, uprooted, and scattered. Peace, Tecumseh argued, was not the answer, for the whites viewed the Indians as animals. If the Sioux failed to unite, he said, they would be forced to live in squalor and misery, dependent on the whites' good graces and on their whiskey to help them forget that they could no longer feed their starving families. He argued that even if they united and failed, which he did not believe would happen, an honorable death on the field of battle was preferable to the isolation and destitution that they certainly faced.

Tecumseh warned that the grandmother of rivers, the Mississippi, would not hold back the white tide. He told the Sioux that the great white chief Thomas Jefferson had purchased from the French the vast lands that belonged to the Indians, and that an expedition of Jefferson's agents (Lewis and Clark) was headed their way. He told them that thirty years earlier the Shawnee had also been at a crossroads with the whites. First came the trappers and traders, then the missionaries and surveyors, and finally a flood of settlers. Even though the Shawnee had fought, their game was killed, their forests decimated, the prairie burned, their villages destroyed, and their people killed. The Kentucky and Ohio country that had been Shawnee homeland for centuries was not part of the Seventeen Fires (the United States). Thus, Tecumseh warned, unless the Indian union he envisioned became strong, unless they put aside their

47

tribal disagreements, unless they realized that all Indians were brothers, there would be no way to keep the whites from grabbing everything the Indians held dear and destroying their way of life.

Tecumseh had a grand vision. He dreamed that some day all Indians would be one people. As his biographer, Allan W. Eckert, wrote, "What he was establishing was an amalgamation—a thrusting aside of jealousies and mistrust and hatreds, and the forging of one people—Indians—who were first and foremost faithful to each other in every respect and unified as a single body, removed from all nationalistic rivalries."[1]

The Sioux Tecumseh visited were impressed by him and his great vision. They even promised that when the time came, they would join with him and the other tribes to fight the common enemy. But Tecumseh was killed at the Battle of the Thames, fighting Americans during the War of 1812. With his death, his lofty vision of Indian unity died also.

In the summer of 1854, the Oglalas and Brulés were once again camped in the Fort Laramie region. While they waited for their annual government handout, they traded buffalo robes from the spring hunt for whiskey, coffee, sugar, and other goods. At the same time, younger warriors continued raiding settlers coming up the Oregon Trail. Curly's Oglala band was now led by Old-Man-Afraid-of-Horses, for the senior chief, Old Smoke, had gone to live at Fort Laramie.

The Brulé camp was headed by Conquering Bear, a handpicked favorite of the whites. For Curly, just entering adolescence, it was to be an exciting summer. Every day, Curly and his friends Hump, Little Hawk, and Lone Bear joined other young braves on excursions to raid wagon trains. These raids were not the bloodcurdling attacks shown in Hollywood films. They were more like the mischief and adventure teenagers of every culture have always sought. The young Sioux would make off with a cow or horse, or sneak into the camp at night to steal a pot or even a gun. There was little danger and even less chance of getting caught. The whites had so much, they hardly ever missed what was taken and rarely chased the youngsters, as the more dangerous enemy tribes might have done. The young Sioux knew that the small contingent of blue-coated soldiers at Fort Laramie could hardly police the entire region, and so the younger Oglala and Brulé braves apparently had the white settlers at their mercy. It was exciting and fun; it gave the restless young men something to do during that warm lazy summer, and nobody would get hurt. Or so the Indians thought.

One day everything changed. A trivial incident on August 17, 1854, sparked a major conflict. A Mormon wagon train was slowly making its way across Sioux territory, passing near the Brulé encampment. A young Minniconjou called Straight Foretop (or High Forehead), who had been staying with the Brulés, watched the Mormon wagons pass. He noticed a lame old cow at the rear of the train and he killed it with a well-placed arrow. Another account says that the cow strayed, ran into the Brulé camp, and Straight Foretop shot it as it lumbered about. Whatever actually happened, the poor cow became supper that night for the young Minniconjou, as the angry Mormon owner came to the Brulé encampment to complain. When he saw hundreds of Indians pointing and shouting at him he became frightened. A Brulé fired a shot over his head and the terrified man fled. The Brulé women laughed heartily at these antics that broke up the monotony of a steamy summer's afternoon.[2]

The Mormon went quickly to Fort Laramie, where he told his tale of the "stolen" cow to the soldiers. The fort was commanded by Lieutenant Hugh B. Fleming, an inexperienced young officer just two years out of West Point. Fort Laramie was not a young officer's dream post. It was hot, dusty, and, worst of all, boring.

Lieutenant Fleming, deciding that the Indians had to be taught a lesson, sent for the Brulé chief, Conquering Bear. The next morning Conquering Bear, who had long cooperated with the whites and tried to maintain the uneasy peace, made his way to Fort Laramie with a number of other Brulé leaders. On the way, the Sioux stopped off at the trading post of James Bordeaux, a trusted French trader who had done business with the Sioux for years. Bordeaux, who was married to a Brulé woman, worried that the Mormon was making trouble. He had earlier offered the man ten dollars for his mangy cow, but the Mormon demanded twenty-five—a huge sum of money in that time. Bordeaux warned his Brulé friends that the Mormon was stirring up the soldiers, saying, "We'll have them Injuns cleaned out like a nest of snakes!"[3]

At Fort Laramie, Conquering Bear and his men were graciously received. Fleming gave the Sioux leaders tobacco, bread, molasses, and coffee, and even laughed about the cow. Conquering Bear told the white soldier that the whole matter was foolish, that the cow was old and lame and that the Indians had always taken stray animals they found on the prairie. But Fleming insisted that the young brave who killed the cow surrender to the authorities at the fort. The amiable Conquering Bear, hoping to end the episode, made a generous offer: the Mormon could come to the Brulé camp and take his pick from the chief's own herd of sixty fine horses. But Fleming would not budge. The Minniconjou "thief," Straight Foretop, had to be given up.

Fleming warned the Brulés that the next day a contingent of soldiers would be sent to arrest the young man, and he ordered the chief to cooperate. The Indians were amazed at the arrogance of the young white soldier-chief with fewer than a hundred men to face a thousand or more Sioux. That night, as Conquering Bear reported the matter to his subchiefs and warriors at the tribal council lodge, those gathered found it hard to comprehend. All this over a cow! A cow whose meat tasted like an "old moccasin!"

Conquering Bear had done his best to explain to Fleming that the man he wanted was not a member of the Brulé band. According to a fur trader who was at the meeting, Fleming insisted, "I want you to bring that man in here." And Conquering Bear had replied, "That man does not belong to my band. He is a Sioux, but he belongs to the Minneconjou band."[4]

Here the white basic misunderstanding of the Sioux, their leadership, and their culture stands out starkly. Indeed, Conquering Bear had been made "the paper chief" by the whites in the Treaty of 1851. But while the whites saw Conquering Bear as the leader of all the Sioux, to the independent bands that made up the Sioux nation, Conquering Bear was only one of many Sioux chieftains.

Although some of the chiefs gathered in Conquering Bear's council lodge complained about the troublemaking young Oglalas and Minniconjous, they knew Conquering Bear could hardly be held accountable for their actions. He had little control over the younger warriors. As Mari Sandoz observed, "They made the old ones, those very fond of the sugar and coffee and whisky [sic] shake to the heel fringe of their mocassins, so afraid were they of losing those soft, white-man things."[5]

Conquering Bear was accompanied to the fort by the Oglala chief, Man-Afraid-of-Horses (later called, Old-Man-Afraid-of-Horses). After the Oglala leader returned to his own camp, word spread that the Brulés were expecting trouble. That night some Oglala boys, anticipating a confrontation between the soldiers and the Indians, gathered to see what would happen. Although most had killed their first buffalo, none had been in combat. Among them were He Dog, Lone Bear, Young-Man-Afraid-of-Horses, (son of Man-Afraid-of-Horses) and Curly (son of Crazy Horse, the Oglala holy man). The boys chattered on into the dark night in anticipation of the next day. They bragged of how, when the time came, they would make war on the Crow and the Snakes and steal horses from the dreaded Pawnee, the traditional enemy of the Sioux.

Curly listened to his friends but said nothing. He had lived all his life with the Oglalas but his mother had been a Brulé, as was his second mother. The day before, while visiting his Brulé cousins, Curly had even been given a piece of hide from the Mormon's cow to stretch over his new war club. Unlike his Oglala comrades, Curly worried that no good would come from a confrontation between soldiers and Brulés. What would happen when the soldiers came to Conquering Bear's village to arrest the Minniconjou? Could soldiers enter a Sioux village and take a warrior away—even a Minniconjou troublemaker—without a fight?[6]

The next morning the soldiers came, commanded by brash, inexperienced, twenty-four-year-old Lieutenant John L. Grattan, a recent graduate of West Point. Grattan had never seen the Sioux in battle and was eager to match his troops against the Indians, for whom he had little respect. He was a heavy drinker who when drunk boasted that with twenty soldiers and a cannon he could defeat the entire Sioux nation.[7] Grattan had often said that the way to break the monotony of frontier duty was to "crack it to the Sioux." Now he would have his chance.[8] He picked up a drunken interpreter, the half-French, half-Iowa Wyuse, and with a column of two horse-drawn wagons filled with twenty-nine soldiers and two field artillery pieces, headed for the Brulé camp to arrest Straight Foretop for stealing a cow.

Young Curly and his friends watched from across the river as the soldiers moved out from the fort. The excited boys raced their ponies back and forth in the water, shouting challenges at the soldiers, who either didn't hear or ignored them. The young Oglalas were finally warned by their chief, Man-Afraid-of-Horses, to return to their camp. So they turned their ponies away from the fort and raced north along the river, in mock battle with the hated white soldiers. Then they galloped to the Oglala camp to spread the news that the soldiers were coming. But Oglala scouts were already out and had reported that thirty soldiers and an interpreter, the trader's son, Lucien (called Wyuse by the Sioux), were on their way to the Sioux stronghold.

To approach the Sioux encampment the soldiers rode over a ridge and, looking down into the broad valley after the dust had cleared from the road, rethought their plan:

This woodcut from the 1850s shows a U.S. Army train crossing the plains.

three Sioux encampments of over six hundred lodges sprawled into the valley, containing as many as twelve hundred warriors. But Grattan was not to be deterred. He ordered his men and wagons forward.[9]

When the soldiers reached the first Sioux encampment, Man-Afraid-of-Horses made it clear that this was not to be an Oglala problem or an Oglala fight. Grattan, probably a little drunk, boldly rode up to the Oglala council lodge and shouted, "Hey, you! You infernal red devils, come out here!" But there was no one in the lodge. Grattan then called for his interpreter. "Tell the damn Indians," he shouted, "they better stay close to their tipis or I'll crack into them." Then Grattan and his detachment rode on, not noticing that the Oglalas had driven their pony herd in close to their camp and that many of the warriors were in full war paint and battle regalia. Nothing like this had ever happened before, and many Oglalas were clearly prepared for a fight, no matter what their chief said.[10]

Grattan next went to Bordeaux's trading post and tried to enlist Jim Bordeaux, who was liked and trusted by the Sioux, to help the soldiers. But the old French trader knew that Grattan was looking for trouble. The Brulés, he informed Grattan, were mourning the death of a beloved old chief, Bull Tail, who had died only the night before. It would be a very bad time, he warned, to go into the Brulé camp. He would not go with him and risk losing the Indians' trust, friendship, and business—not to mention his life.[11]

As the soldiers approached the Brulé camp, Grattan's drunken interpreter, Wyuse, whipped and spurred his horse, whooping and shouting insults at the Sioux. The soldiers, Wyuse screamed abusively, would give the Sioux new ears to understand the words of the whites. The Brulé women, aware of the impending danger, grabbed their children and moved them away from the camp toward the bank of the nearby river. They were followed by Brulé warriors stripped to their breechcloths and ready to do battle if necessary. Oglalas and Minniconjou warriors also joined with the mounted Brulés along the trail that led to the camp. Red Cloud, Black Twin, and his brother, No Water, and other famous Sioux warriors were present and ready for trouble.

Still, the Brulé chief, Conquering Bear, felt the matter could be settled. He went out to greet Grattan, planning to bargain with the Americans and was not even wearing war paint. He hoped the soldiers would sit down, have a smoke, and settle the difficulty peacefully. Wyuse continued to shout that he would cut out the hearts of the Sioux and eat them for breakfast as the gathered Brulé chieftains looked on in stunned, apprehensive silence.

Grattan remained adamant. He insisted that Conquering Bear deliver the Minniconjou, Straight Foretop. Following custom, Conquering Bear consulted with the young warrior, who refused to give himself up. Conquering Bear and Grattan met for over a half hour, as the officer's threats grew louder and more insistent. As the meeting went on, many of the younger Sioux boys, including Curly and his friends, watched from the surrounding hills.

Conquering Bear once more attempted to conciliate. He offered a good mule from his own herd for the butchered cow. Then he offered five good horses from the herds of five of his men. But Grattan had not come for mules or horses. He wanted a prisoner or he wanted blood.

Conquering Bear again approached Straight Foretop, who was standing with his gun and bow and arrow in the doorway of a nearby lodge. The young man again refused to surrender. He had seen three of his people killed the year before by white soldiers in an argument over a boat. He was not going with the whites without a fight. Conquering Bear knew that if he gave up the Minniconjou, many of his people would be angry. But if he refused, many might die. Finally, the old chief agreed to surrender the Minniconjou. But first, he would have to follow Sioux custom and get his own gun since he would now be approaching Straight Foretop as an enemy. Perhaps the drunken Wyuse didn't explain Conquering Bear's words accurately. Perhaps he did. Whatever the interpreter said, Grattan's face grew redder and redder with anger.

As the old chief turned toward his lodge, Grattan barked out an angry order. A shot was fired and the brother of Conquering Bear fell with blood gushing from his mouth. Then Grattan foolishly ordered his wagon guns to open fire. Cannon fire ripped through the Brulé camp as the other chiefs scattered. Conquering Bear, stood his ground, urging the Indians to remain calm and not charge the soldiers. But within seconds Conquering Bear was down in a pool of blood, wounded by nine bullets.

The Brulés poured out of their lodges. The Oglalas waiting in the hills galloped their ponies down into the village. In minutes the battle was over. The Minniconjou, Straight Foretop, fired his rifle through the cannon smoke and shot Grattan. The furious Sioux pounced on the fallen officer and hacked him to pieces. A hail of arrows and war lances finished off the soldiers. Some tried to get back to the main road but they soon were down, overwhelmed after the first charge by the enraged warriors. One soldier, Private John Cuddy, survived, but died a few days later from his wounds.

Wyuse, now terrified, frantically galloped up toward the road, but his horse stumbled and fell. In panic, he mistakenly ran into the death lodge of Bull Tail, where the angry Sioux followed him and dragged him out crying. The interpreter's own brother-in-law struck him with a war club and slashed him from his ankle to his waist as a dozen other warriors finished him off.[12]

As soon as the rampaging warriors left, Curly and his friends crept into the Brulé village. Curly stared down with contempt at Wyuse's mutilated body. His blood rose and he felt dizzy with anger. At that moment he wanted, more than anything, to kill whites and make them pay for their actions. After ritually insulting the dead body of the despised interpreter, Curly jumped on his pony and galloped back to the Oglala camp.[13]

The Sioux warriors, stirred into a frenzy, arrived at the Bordeaux trading post. Aware of what had taken place, the trader hid all his whiskey and prayed that the Indians would not treat him as their enemy. Bordeaux survived the night by giving the Indians whatever they wanted from his store. Hoping that cooler heads would prevail, he advised one Sioux leader, "If they do no more damage the Great Father may forgive it. They have some reason for fighting the soldiers who come and kill their chief before their eyes, but if they burn his fort he will send a hundred wagon guns; the soldiers will come thick as the grasshoppers in summer to fight them, to butcher the women and children."[14]

The angry Sioux began arguing among themselves. The younger warriors wanted to ride on to Fort Laramie, kill all the soldiers, and drive the whites out of Sioux territory forever. The elder men, led by Man-Afraid-of-Horses who still thought about the yearly government allotment, wanted to head north, forgo the whites' gifts for the year, and hope for things to cool down. Perhaps, they reasoned, the whites would see that Grattan was the victim of his own arrogance and stupidity.[15]

In the end, the Oglala and Brulé women decided the matter. The women packed up the camps and began the journey north. Since it was a warrior's obligation to protect the helpless who were now moving across the prairie without any protection, the Sioux warriors returned to their families.

Could the Sioux, after this initial bloody encounter, have beaten back subsequent intrusions by the whites and, as Tecumseh once hoped, been united against a common enemy? The answer is no. Historian Stephen E. Ambrose believes the failure of the Sioux to take advantage of their victory against the soldiers was inevitable. The Sioux could not function as a disciplined military cadre and, at the same time, freely roam the prairie. The Sioux, between their hatred of the encroaching whites and the freedom that was part of their life and culture, chose freedom.[16]

Since Curly's mother was a Brulé, Curly went to live among them as the Brulés moved rapidly east toward western Nebraska, carrying the dying Conquering Bear with them. As the band traveled, Curly had time to reflect upon the Grattan massacre. He had just turned thirteen and he had seen many men brutally killed in battle. Conquering Bear was dying, and one day Curly caught a glimpse of the wounded old chief. He was standing behind his friend Hump when he saw what "looked like a skull from the prairie with the yellow skin still on it, the eye holes almost as deep and empty, and all around the smell of death."[17]

Young Curly was deeply affected by what he saw. It was now time, he felt, to take his place in the band as a full-fledged warrior. But first, like many great warriors before him, Curly sought his vision quest—the mystical dream that gives a Sioux fighting man the power to guide his destiny. Without a vision, the Sioux believed, a warrior would always be powerless. With a vision, he would be touched by the sacred and spiritual forces that would remain with him all his life. And so, without the approval of anyone, or even the ritual purification and lectures from a Sioux holy man, Curly headed his pony out from the Brulé camp to a bluff overlooking a river to seek his vision.[18]

In the meantime, word of the Grattan massacre had spread over the frontier. Frightened settlers clamored for protection. The American government had made no judgment on the wisdom or legality of Grattan's foolish attempt to cow the Sioux. Rather, the government was concerned only with the protection of settlers along the Oregon Trail and with teaching the Sioux a lesson.

As the army inspector sent to investigate the Grattan massacre reported, "[t]he time has now fully arrived for teaching these barbarians . . . how to appreciate and respect the power, the justice, the generosity and the magnanimity of the United States."[19]

For a young Sioux seeking a sacred vision in the wilderness, those words would have an impact beyond anything he or his people could imagine. The whites had been streaming into Sioux territory since 1842—the year Curly was born. Now, in his thirteenth year, Curly and his people faced a power they neither knew nor understood. In a hundred and fifty years the whites had pushed farther and farther west, mercilessly pressing the Native Americans in their path. The Indians, whose resistance was often too little too late, were no match for the advancing whites in any area except for raw courage. By the mid-1850s, the whites had firmly planted themselves on the border of the Great Plains, and they were there to stay. They would never be pushed back.

However, a young Oglala boy could not see into the future. To Curly, what mattered was the past. The old ways of his people were to be cherished, protected, and, if necessary, fought for. He could not know that the old ways of the Oglalas and Brulés were numbered and the last days of the great Sioux Nation were on the horizon.

CHAPTER FOUR

CRAZY HORSE:
SEEKER OF VISIONS

For three days Curly remained on the craggy butte above the Platte River, waiting for his vision. To keep awake he placed stones between his toes and piles of pebbles under his back. Finally, on the third day, weak and dizzy from fasting, Curly decided he had not prepared adequately. He rose to get his pony that was tethered at the bank of the river; he would seek a vision on another occasion. But Curly was so weak that he then either fainted, or fell into a deep sleep.

During his sleep a vision came in a hazy dream. A man on horseback floated toward him. As the man came closer the horse changed colors. The man wore blue leggings and a white buckskin shirt, and a single feather was fastened in his brown hair that flowed down to his waist. He appeared to be held back several times by his own people, who grabbed him from behind and clasped his arms. But the man shook them off and continued forward, while storm clouds rolled and thunder clapped. As the man came closer, Curly could see a zigzag of lightning across his cheek and hailstones on his body that had been suddenly stripped down to a breechcloth for fighting.[1]

The man told Curly never to wear a warbonnet or to braid his horse's tail, although this was the Sioux custom.

In a traditional Sioux ritual, a dead warrior is wrapped in a buffalo robe and placed high in a tree overlooking the Valley of the Running Water.

He said that if Curly brushed lines and streaks of dirt over his horse, he would not have to paint his horse (another Sioux custom) before going into battle. If Curly then brushed the dirt over himself, he could never be killed in battle by an enemy bullet. He also told Curly to remain selfless and to refrain from taking anything for himself.[2]

Curly awakened startled to find his father and Hump standing over him. They were angry because Curly had gone off into the wilderness alone, unmindful of the dangerous Pawnee and Crow war parties raiding in the area. They were even angrier when Curly told them he had gone off to seek a vision. How could an Oglala warrior, they scolded, have sought his vision without proper preparations?

Curly didn't tell them of his vision. He returned with them to his father's lodge where he was given a little soup and sent off to sleep. Curly remained silent, angry that everyone treated him like a child when his vision prophesied that he would become a great warrior and a leader of his people. Why didn't they understand that he was destined for great things?

However, the episode was forgotten in the events of the following day. The dying Conquering Bear called Man-Afraid-of-Horses, Curly's father, and other leaders to his lodge. Conquering Bear told them of his hopes for the future. He said that the treaty with the whites had been good, for the Sioux would receive their yearly allotment for fifty-five years. Conquering Bear foresaw great change. The Sioux, he hoped, would give up warring with their traditional enemies and honor the 1851 treaty by protecting the Holy Road (the Oregon Trail). He designated the protesting Man-Afraid-of-Horses to be the next leader of the Teton branch of the Sioux Nation. And then the beloved old Brulé chief died.[3]

The Brulés wrapped Conquering Bear's body in a buffalo robe and placed it on a traditional scaffold (the Sioux, like many Indians, honored their dead by placing them above ground). They placed his bow and shield with him as he was given a high spot above the plains, overlooking what the Sioux called the Valley of the Running Water. After a few days of mourning, Brulé life returned to normal. The tribe had to plan for the coming winter, so the band moved off in search of the buffalo herd.

Curly spent quiet fall days in his village, and spent evenings at his father's lodge fire with his younger brother Little Hawk, teasing their older sister. The trouble with the whites of the previous summer seemed far away.[4] That fall Curly was the first to find the great buffalo herd that would provide meat and clothing for the winter. On the night after the hunt, Hump sang praises for his young protégé around the Brulé campfire. Even though Curly's voice had never been heard in council he had become, Hump sang, "the ears of his people." That night, many in camp called out Curly's name for the feat of locating the great herd that meant the difference between life and death during the cruel plains winter.[5]

That November some Brulé warriors, including Curly's uncle, Spotted Tail, decided to make war on the whites to avenge the death of Conquering Bear. Although Conquering Bear had pleaded that the peace with the whites be kept, Spotted Tail and his small group made their own decision, apart from the larger Brulé or Oglala bands and from the Sioux in general.

Spotted Tail and his Brulés attacked a mail wagon on the Oregon Trail, killing two drivers and wounding a passenger while stealing $20,000, mostly in paper money, gold, and silver. Some of the gold and silver was spent at the Bordeaux trading post. But the Indians were unfamiliar with paper banknotes. They rolled some banknotes into cigarettes and smoked them. The rest they tossed into the air and watched the wind carry them away. When Jim Bordeaux told them of the money's value, they laughed again. The whites were strange indeed, putting value on useless bits of paper.[6]

That winter and the following spring of 1855, the Brulés were joined by some young Oglala and Minniconjou braves in a series of raids along the Oregon Trail. The Sioux war parties were actually more of a nuisance than a threat. They killed no whites, but they stole horses and cattle as if they were raiding their ancient enemies, the Crow or Pawnee. While the Oglalas, led by Man-Afraid-of-Horses, stayed far to the north of the Fort Laramie region and had little to do with the attacks along the Oregon Trail, many of the younger braves, including Curly, joined the Brulés in the raids. To the whites, the problem was confusing. While some Oglala leaders spoke of peace, many of their young men were joining the Brulés in attacking whites. The American authorities could not tell which of the Sioux were violating the treaty. And so whenever there was a raid, they blamed all Sioux.[7]

To remedy the situation and to gain some form of retribution for the Grattan massacre, in August 1855 the Army sent Colonel William Harney and a platoon of 1,300 soldiers to discipline the Sioux and to secure the road for white travelers and settlers along the Platte River. The United States Army made no distinction between hostile or friendly Sioux; Harney's orders were to terrorize any Sioux he met.[8] Harney had established a reputation as an Indian fighter fighting the Seminoles, when he hanged thirteen of their chiefs. As he set out with his large force, Harney remarked, "By God, I am for war—no peace."[9]

That summer, as the Harney expedition was forming, Curly was experiencing the joy and adventure of becoming a young, respected Oglala warrior. In July 1855 Curly joined a Brulé raiding party of a few older warriors and a larger group of young braves and boys hoping for their first real battle and the chance to steal a few good ponies. The Brulés had targeted a Pawnee village and a large Omaha hunting party. The Omaha, a tribe that often traveled west in summer to hunt buffalo, always had good horses.

The Brulés split up. Some went down the Loup River to raid a Pawnee village. The others, including Curly, hit the Omaha encampment at night and got away with some of their finest horses. The next day, with many Omaha warriors out looking for their stolen horses, the Sioux swept down on the unprotected camp and killed three Omahas. Curly was in the thick of the fight when he spotted an Omaha brave sneaking through a patch of brush. He drew his bow and fired an arrow and could see that he had made a good hit. Elated by his first enemy kill, Curly rushed over to take his victim's scalp as a trophy of battle when, to his horror, he saw that he had killed a woman.

While it was no great shame for a Sioux brave to kill a woman (the shame was actually on the warrior who allowed his woman to be killed), Curly was filled with revulsion. He felt sick and did not scalp the woman. As the war party made their way home, the braves teased Curly about losing his first scalp. But Curly did not care. He could not feel good about killing a woman—even an enemy woman.[10]

In early September, as Curly rode back to join his family in the Fort Laramie region, the Harney expedition reached the Ash Hollow village of the Brulé chief Little Thunder, alongside a creek about a hundred miles north of the Platte River. Little Thunder had been one of the Sioux leaders who counseled restraint after the killing of Chief Conquering Bear. He was known to the government Indian agents as a man of peace. Even though the trader Jim Bordeaux warned the Brulés that the soldiers were coming, the friendly government Indian agent sent word that Little Thunder would be foolish to move his people. All Little Thunder had to do was show the soldiers that he was for peace.[11]

Perhaps that is what Little Thunder wanted to hear, because the Brulés had no desire to move south of the Platte to join the four hundred Sioux lodges set up under the protection of the new Indian agent, Thomas Twiss. Twiss ordered the Sioux to come into the Laramie encampment or be considered hostile. But Twiss's agents gave the Brulés under Little Thunder confusing messages. Besides, Little Thunder was convinced that the soldiers knew of him and that he meant no harm or disrespect by staying put. The Brulés had enjoyed a good buffalo hunt that summer and rather than spend weeks of travel, they wanted time to get the buffalo meat and skins ready for the coming winter.[12]

On September 2, 1855, Colonel Harney and his troops reached the vicinity of Little Thunder's camp. They came upon a wagon train that had been harassed by the Brulés. Although Little Thunder's people hadn't actually attacked the settlers, they had demanded guns and ammunition from them. So the Sioux were alert to the possibility of trouble. But Little Thunder had no idea of what a powerful force of infantry, cavalry, and artillery could do. Harney, Little Thunder believed, would be as easy to defeat as Grattan. But Little Thunder forgot that there had been over 2,000 Brulés and Oglalas against Grattan's tiny force, while Little Thunder had only about one hundred warriors to face Harney's troops.

On September 3, Harney surrounded Little Thunder's camp. He sent his cavalry through the hills to cut off the far end of the village, while he moved his infantry and artillery into place to attack Little Thunder from the front. Little Thunder was not much of a military man. Many of his warriors, including the party that Curly was with that summer, were scattered across the plains. Worse, Little Thunder had sent out no scouts and thus the Brulés did not know of Harney's aggressive intentions or even of his presence until too late.

Initially, both sides agreed to a council. But the meeting was a sham. Little Thunder wanted to buy time to get his women and children away; Harney wanted time to maneuver his troops into position. Little Thunder rode out from his village with Curly's uncle, Spotted Tail, by his side. The Indians carried a white flag. At the meeting with Harney, the Brulé chief professed friendship for the whites. Even as they talked, Harney's men were moving to surround the Sioux camp.

Harney told the Brulé leaders that he had been sent to arrest the Sioux who had killed Grattan and his men. He demanded that they be surrendered immediately. Little Thunder and Spotted Tail, finally aware that Harney was stalling to get his troops into position, hastily galloped back toward the Brulé village to warn that an attack was imminent. But it was too late. Harney's infantry was behind them and the mounted cavalry cut them off from the village. The brutal Battle of the Blue Water began.[13]

The soldiers opened up on the village with artillery and then charged in from two directions with drawn sabers. Eighty-six Sioux were killed and Harney's troops captured seventy women and children, marching them off in chains while singing,

> We did not make a blunder,
> We rubbed out Little Thunder
> And we sent him to the other side of Jordan.[14]

The battle lasted little more than a half hour and it was a slaughter. Little Thunder and Spotted Tail were seriously wounded. Spotted Tail's small daughter was among those killed. Returning that night from the summer hunt with his Brulé relatives and friends, Curly reached Little Thunder's village in the midst of a thunderstorm. Seeing smoke, Curly spurred his horse toward the camp. As he rode in, the acrid smell of gunpowder burned his nostrils. The sky flashed with lightning, and smoke rose from the devastation around him. Curly was sick to his stomach. He walked his jittery horse up a hill and gazed with disbelief at the dead bodies of Indians all about him. The soldiers had hacked the Sioux children with swords and shot many women. Other bodies lay torn apart by the explosions of Harney's heavy artillery. Walking farther, Curly found the sister of a friend. Her dead body had been shamed and mutilated by the soldiers. In the past, the Sioux had considered eight or ten casualties in a battle a disastrous loss. What Curly saw would remain etched in his mind.

Curly's sickness gave way to rage. How could this have happened? How could the whites have attacked a village that had not made war against them? His angry thoughts reverted to his vision. As the lightning flashed and the thunder clapped, Curly knew its meaning. He knew what to do with his life. He would lead his people against the whites.

Later, as Curly rode hard to catch up to the escaping remnants of Little Thunder's camp, he came upon a Cheyenne woman and her just-born infant hiding in a gully under a buffalo robe. Nearby, Curly found her son, a small boy shot through the chest. They had been spending the summer with Little Thunder's band. Her husband had been killed trying to protect his wife and wounded son. She carried her dying son as far as she could before going into labor. Curly tied the Cheyenne, Yellow Woman, and her newborn child to a travois (a horse-drawn carrier used by the Plains Indians to transport goods and people) and took them with him. He soon caught up with his people in a well-guarded camp. They fed Curly and described the massacre of Little Thunder's camp. They also took in the Cheyenne woman and her baby.[15]

Word of the Ash Hollow tragedy spread across the prairie. The Sioux, terrified of the power of the white soldiers, fled to the sanctuary of their sacred Black Hills in the Dakotas. As Harney and his force made their way back to Fort Laramie, they never saw a single Indian.

In March of 1856, at a council at Fort Laramie, Harney proposed a new peace treaty to the Sioux chiefs. He agreed to release his prisoners, resume payments of the annuity (which he had held up), and protect the Sioux from "impositions" from white settlers. In return, Harney expected the Sioux to turn over the warriors who had been raiding the wagon trains, to return the money stolen from the mail wagon, and to stop harassing settlers along the Platte River road. Although the Indians agreed to Harney's terms, the new treaty never became law because the United States Senate, preoccupied with the problems of slavery, hardly had time to worry about Indian troubles on the far-off plains.[16]

The Sioux leaders, impressed by Harney's military might, agreed to his terms, and Spotted Tail and the others guilty of the mail-wagon robbery did what no Sioux had ever done—surrendered voluntarily to the white authorities. Curly watched in disbelief as Spotted Tail and his Brulé friends endured the humiliation of being transported down the Holy Road in heavy chains. Standing amid his people on land that had once belonged to the mighty Sioux, Curly listened as the women wept over the possibility of never seeing their loved ones again. He wondered whether it would not be better to die fighting the whites than to surrender so meekly.[17] However, the Sioux were not planning a quiet acceptance. The chiefs secretly sent out runners to every band, and called for a great Sioux council the following summer at Bear Butte, a region north of the Black Hills. The Sioux chiefs hoped to unite against white advancement into their territory.[18]

That winter Curly rejoined the Oglalas and his family. He had not seen them for a year and it was good, even in such a troubled time, to be home again. It was a hard winter with very deep snows, making it difficult for the various Sioux bands to visit each other. Walkers—young men on snowshoes who traveled from village to village—were sent out to keep each Sioux band abreast of the news. Initially, there was no word of what had happened to Spotted Tail and the other Brulés held at the new fort on the Missouri River. Many of the younger warriors were restless and angry. Hump spoke the question in the minds of many younger Sioux braves that winter: "Is this thing that the whites call peace worth so much?"[19]

The following fall, Spotted Tail and the other Brulés were released from Fort Leavenworth to return to their people. But Curly, who visited his Brulé relatives often that fall and winter, noticed that Spotted Tail had changed. He seemed broken by his experience in the whites' jail. Spotted Tail warned the Oglalas and the Brulés that the white soldiers were as thick as a cloud of locusts and that the only road for the Sioux to pursue was peace. "It is useless to fight; they are too many. We must keep the peace," Spotted Tail said.[20]

In the summer of 1857, when Curly was fifteen, he had already seen much suffering among his people and their friends, the Cheyennes, at the hands of the white soldiers. Curly spent the winter of 1856–57 visiting Yellow Woman's Cheyenne tribe, where he was a hero for having saved the niece of the tribe's famous medicine man, Ice. Curly took part in a number of minor skirmishes with the white soldiers that winter and spring. As he headed north to attend the Great Council meeting in Bear Butte that had been called for the seven tribes of the Teton Sioux, many thoughts raced through his mind. The Sioux, he felt, seemed to be giving up to the whites too easily. They had seen the Cheyenne killed by small groups of whites because their numbers were few and they always fought alone.

News came from the east that the whites were driving the Indians onto reservations. Such a catastrophe would soon, Curly believed, arrive on the plains unless the Sioux banded together to drive away the whites. Perhaps at the Great Teton Council the chiefs would finally unite the tribes.[21]

What Curly saw that summer along the banks of the Belle Fourche River had to seem encouraging. Between 5,000 and 7,500 Sioux gathered in the Black Hills, in an historic attempt to cope with the rapacious whites. All the Teton Dakota tribes attended the Great Teton Council: the Oglala, Minniconjou, Sans Arc, Blackfeet, Two Kettles, and Hunkpapa, a wild Sioux band from the north who had seen little battle with the dreaded whites. For the first time Curly saw the leaders of his people gathered together to discuss a problem. The Hunkpapa chief Four Horns and his young nephew Sitting Bull, who was already a famous warrior, were there; Long Mandan of the Two Kettles, Crow Feather of the Sans Arcs, the rising Oglala chiefs Man-Afraid-of-Horses and Red Cloud, and the seven-foot Minniconjou warrior, Touch-the-Clouds, were gathered there too.[22]

The Sioux, heartened by their large numbers, "solemnly pledged to each other not to permit further encroachment from the whites."[23] But the Grand Teton Council of 1857 accomplished little. The great meeting had the air of a summer harvest festival, not that of a conference of people whose way of life and existence was threatened. There was much feasting, dancing, and gossiping. Curly was reunited with his family, his friend Hump, and Curly's growing brother, Little Hawk, already a veteran of two war parties at the age of twelve. And, for the first time, Curly appeared to pay attention to the Indian girls. He seemed interested in Black Buffalo Woman, a pretty young niece of the Oglala chief Red Cloud.[24]

That fall the Teton Sioux returned to their traditional buffalo hunt and then went back to set up their winter camps. The various Sioux bands, ever faithful to tribal custom, went their separate ways. Historian Stephen E. Ambrose laments the Sioux Council's lost opportunity:

> They had not elected a head chief or indeed done anything to provide for an institutional basis for resistance. No generals were appointed, no scouts organized, no system for exchanging information set up, no provision made for arming the warriors with guns instead of bow and arrow. . . . Nor was there any discussion on how to fight the whites. Nothing but promises.[25]

Immediately after the Great Council, Curly went off with his father, Crazy Horse. They made camp on a peaceful butte overlooking a sheltered valley and a meandering stream. Together they built a sweat lodge and purified themselves while fasting and talking. Finally, confident that he could confide in his father, Curly told Crazy Horse of his vision. Crazy Horse felt certain that his son was destined to be a great leader. "Somewhere a good man must rise from the young ones among us," Crazy Horse told Curly. "One who has had no part in the old troubles. It will not be enough for him to speak words of wisdom if he cannot give the people ears to hear and hearts to make them strong against the power of the white man's favor. He must be one who does great deeds for the young to see, great deeds for the people. It will take a very big, a very strong man, one the people can see standing above the others." The leader Crazy Horse spoke of would need "great vision, one that drives him straight as the bowstring sends the arrow...."[26]

But the road ahead, the father warned, would be paved with grave danger. "It would take a great man to save the people now, a very great man, and many will hate him, and many try to get him killed," Crazy Horse said.[27] Curly understood that his father's interpretation of his vision meant that Crazy Horse saw his son as a rare Sioux leader who would play a role in the destiny of his struggling people.

A few days later Curly and his father joined a group of Hunkpapas and Minniconjous hunting buffalo west of the Black Hills. Since the buffalo had not yet grown the full coats that the Indians used for their winter robes and blankets, the Sioux herded the animals, posting scouts to the south in order to keep the great herd together. The fall days in the Black Hills were uneventful until a young American army surveyor, Lieutenant Gouverneur K. Warren, stumbled upon the Sioux hunting camp. Some of the younger warriors were angry that another white had violated the treaty and invaded their sacred Black Hills. They wanted to kill Warren and his men. But Bear Ribs, a Minniconjou chief, held them back. Even though the Teton Sioux had agreed at the Great Council to stop the whites from intruding further onto Sioux lands, Bear Ribs and some of the older chiefs knew an attack on Warren and his men would draw Harney's fury.

Lieutenant Warren, an 1850 graduate of West Point, was only twenty-six. But he listened to the Sioux complaints sympathetically as they warned him to turn back to avoid driving away the buffalo herd. After meeting with Bear Ribs, Warren marched back to Bear Butte and then east, away from the Black Hills. The Sioux allowed him to proceed peacefully, thus avoiding a confrontation with the whites that winter.[28]

In the following summer of 1858, when Curly was sixteen, he joined his brother Little Hawk, Hump, and some friends in a war party that headed to the far west. The Oglalas traveled into the land of the Shoshone (called Snakes by the Sioux) and the Arapaho, in what is today central Wyoming. In an extended battle with a party of Arapaho, Curly fought bravely, risking his life in a hail of bullets and arrows. It appeared as if the prophecy had been correct and Curly was invincible in battle. At one point he killed two Arapaho warriors. He shot one with an arrow, as his enemy pointed a gun at him. Curly shot the second with his pistol as the Arapaho rode him down. But in the heat of the battle, Curly forgot the prophecy. He jumped from his pony to take his victims' scalps and the horse panicked, jerked loose, and galloped away. As Curly scalped the second warrior he was hit in the leg by an Arapaho arrow. He had to run down the hill on foot in order to escape. That night as Hump cut the iron arrow from Curly's leg and dressed the wound, Curly told Hump that he had been wounded because he had violated the prophecy. He was not to take anything—not even an enemy scalp.[29]

When they returned to their village the Oglalas celebrated the war party with a victory dance. The Oglalas had killed four Arapaho enemies, counted eight coups (a coup was touching an enemy in battle and was considered a great accomplishment and a brave feat for a warrior), stolen some fine horses, and lost no warriors of their own. It had been a successful foray. That night, each warrior rose in front of the fire in the camp circle to tell of his bravery to loud cheering and approval from the gathered Oglala people.

Only Curly remained silent. Twice his friends pushed him into the circle and twice he backed away. His father and mother were there, as was the young girl, Black Buffalo Woman, who had caught Curly's fancy. But Curly remained silent, even though Hump and Little Hawk couldn't understand why Curly refused to brag about his deeds.

That night Curly couldn't sleep. It wasn't because of his wound. His father redressed his leg with herbs cooked in an old stone bowl. He was troubled. Finally, at sunrise, just as his village awakened, Curly fell into an exhausted sleep. When he woke up his mother gave him some soup. Then his father, who had learned of his son's bravery, put on his ceremonial blanket and walked through the Oglala village chanting and singing. By the time Crazy Horse returned to his lodge, a double line of people were behind him. Young men, old men, children, chiefs, and women followed Crazy Horse as he sang,

> *My son has been against the people of unknown tongue,*
> *He has done a brave thing;*
> *For this I give him a new name, the name of his father,*
> *and of many fathers before him—*
> *I give him a great name,*
> *I call him Crazy Horse.*[30]

After that, Crazy Horse's father was known as Worm. And the Oglala boy Curly took the name that would be forever remembered in Sioux folklore and history. Curly had become the great warrior of his prophecy, Crazy Horse.[31]

The years before the whites arrived were plentiful; in this photograph Indian women cure buffalo hides by drying them in the sun.

CHAPTER FIVE

SAND CREEK LIGHTS
UP THE PLAINS

Kill and scalp all, big and little; nits make lice.
—Colonel John M. Chivington (1864)

The years between 1858 and 1865 were largely happy for the Oglala Sioux. The Oglalas ranged to the north of the Platte River, living in relative freedom from military interference until 1862. The Americans, preoccupied by the Civil War east of the Mississippi, paid little attention to the Indians on the western frontier of the Great Plains.[1]

The Oglala Sioux returned to many of their old ways, from before the white settlers had intruded along the Oregon Trail. As historian Stephen E. Ambrose writes,

> *Those were fat times for the Oglalas, the smell of roasting buffalo ribs rising from their campfires, plenty of good skins for their lodges, the horse herds growing every year at the expense of the Crows and Shoshonis. War parties went out each summer, giving ambitious young braves opportunities to count coup, steal horses, and win honors. It was glorious warfare, for the most part, exactly suited to the Oglala style. Nearly all the fighting was done in summer....[2]*

They were no longer begging from the whites along the Oregon Trail, they were no longer drinking themselves silly with the whites' whiskey, and they were no longer ravaged by the whites' terrible diseases. The Santee Sioux, who still lived in Minnesota, became involved in a fierce war with white settlers, but that seemed far away to Crazy Horse's people and the other Teton bands. The Santee Sioux, resentful of years of mistreatment by whites and dependent reservation life, raged along the Minnesota frontier, killing 750 white settlers.

The Santee uprising was crushed by the head of the Minnesota militia, General Henry Sibley. The poorly equipped Santee were quickly defeated, and Sibley condemned 303 Sioux leaders to death. When the execution orders reached President Abraham Lincoln, a veteran of the Black Hawk War in Illinois who had some sympathy for the Indians, he reviewed the case of each condemned Santee and eventually commuted most of the sentences. However, thirty-eight Santee were hanged in Mankato, Minnesota, in the largest mass execution in American history.[3]

The western tribes gave refuge to their Minnesota relatives who were driven from their lands into Canada or into the Dakota territory. Still, it appeared that the whites were far more troubled than the Indians. White settlers and miners, uneasy because Civil War activity left them with little military protection along the frontier, feared trouble. And the local white militias, who despised and feared the Plains Indians, were itching to fight. Gradually, news of the Santee uprising filtered into the camps of the Oglalas and other Teton Sioux and the Indians became apprehensive as well.[4]

By 1863 General Alfred Sully was in pursuit of the Santee who had fled the Minnesota frontier to join Teton relatives on the plains. The army made little distinction between a Santee or a Teton. A Sioux was a Sioux. And an Indian was an Indian.

By the end of 1863 most of the Santee had either been killed or captured. But there was another reason the troops had been sent after the Santee. Gold had been discovered near Virginia City in Montana. The real reason for chasing the Santee so relentlessly into Teton lands was to ensure that the roads through the Powder River country would be safe so that whites could reach the new mining claims in Montana.

So General Sully forced the Tetons into battle. And the Tetons were more than happy to oblige. Chief Bear Ribs, who sought peace with the whites, was murdered, and by the end of 1863 the commissioner of Indian affairs, William Dole, was complaining that the United States "had upon [its] hands, in addition to the great rebellion, an Indian war of no mean proportion."[5]

During this time Crazy Horse was maturing into a leader of his people, earning a name as a great warrior among the Oglalas. In these years Crazy Horse roamed across the plains to visit other Sioux bands and stay with his Cheyenne friends. He was a free spirit, hunting, fighting, and living his life as he thought it was meant to be lived. Almost every summer he went out with Sioux war parties. In these years the Oglalas fought Crows, Shoshones, and the Arapaho, and actually drove the Crows and the Shoshones from the Powder River country, taking over some of the best buffalo ranges for themselves.[6]

Crazy Horse's prowess in battle was legendary and, true to his vision, he gave away most of the horses he brought back from raids. Other Oglala warriors clamored to join his war party for they believed it would be profitable and word had spread that Crazy Horse did not leave dead or wounded comrades on the field of battle. By 1865, when he was twenty-three, Crazy Horse was a well-recognized war chief among the Oglalas. As Crazy Horse's friend He Dog recalled many years later, "Crazy Horse always led his men himself when they went into battle, and he kept well in front of them. He headed many charges."[7]

Around this time, during his early twenties, two significant events occurred: Crazy Horse fell deeply in love, and he became a "Shirt-Wearer." Courtship and dating in Sioux culture were very different than in today's America.

The roles played by women in Sioux society, with a few notable exceptions, were those of homemaker and mother. Indian women were considered property of their men. Thus, in a legal and technical sense, they had little voice in choosing their husbands, although they ordinarily had the right to approve their mates. There was little chance for intimacy between young people in Sioux culture before marriage. Chastity and faithfulness were the watchwords of Sioux sexual relations in and out of marriage.

A young Sioux brave, interested in a young Sioux maiden, was permitted to visit her in front of her tipi, where they stood in full view of the girl's family. It was customary for the young warrior to cover his prospective bride and himself from view with his buffalo robe. In that way, with even their heads covered from prying family eyes, the young couple could at least converse privately. If a prospective suitor was acceptable, the girl's family was given presents, usually horses, to seal the marriage bargain. The presents had little actual meaning since once the marriage was arranged, her family gave gifts of equal value back to the suitor's family.

In Sioux culture, marriage was a serious matter even though there was no formal ceremony. All that was required was for the young man and woman to spend the night together. Although divorce was not unheard of, and was easily accomplished, it was rare. Sioux marriages, once consented to by the girl's father, were usually unions that lasted for life. Crazy Horse's father and his mother, for example, remained together for fifty years. In some respects the Sioux were not unlike their nineteenth-century proper Victorian counterparts.[8]

Black Buffalo Woman, the young niece of the rising chief Red Cloud, was very popular and had many young braves pursuing her. Crazy Horse often rode to her lodge and waited patiently in line with as many as a dozen other young men before he could cover her with his buffalo blanket and steal a few precious moments of privacy. Among her other suitors was No Water, a brave from a prominent

Oglala family. His brother Black Twin was a member of the powerful tribal council.

In early 1862 Crazy Horse was set up for a fall. Red Cloud sent word around the camp that he would lead a large war party against the Crows. Among the warriors he invited to come along were No Water, his brother Black Twin, Hump, Crazy Horse, and his brother Little Hawk. Such an invitation was a great honor and Crazy Horse accepted. Just before the war party set out, No Water complained of a toothache. A toothache before battle was a dangerous omen, so No Water stayed behind. Two weeks later, when Red Cloud's war party returned with many enemy scalps and horses, a scout sent out to meet the party gave Crazy Horse the news that No Water had taken Black Buffalo Woman as his bride.

Red Cloud seems heavily involved in what was, in effect, a conspiracy. Wary of young Crazy Horse's rising popularity among the Oglalas, Red Cloud acted to take the wind out of the young warrior's sails. At the same time, this marriage that united two powerful Oglala families could help the ambitious Red Cloud. Politics, among the Sioux, too, was often a powerful force.

Crazy Horse was disconsolate. Instead of joining the celebration for the returning war party, he took to his family's lodge for three days. There, no one would dare disturb him; not even his father. Then, still filled with despair, Crazy Horse packed his war gear and rode out alone toward the country of the Crows. No one knows what he did and Crazy Horse never spoke of it. But when he returned, he had a new rifle which he gave to Little Hawk, and a pair of soldier's binoculars. He also had two Crow scalps that he threw to the village dogs. No Water and Black Buffalo Woman, aware of Crazy Horse's grief and anger, avoided him. Murder over a lost or stolen love was not uncommon among the Sioux.

Some months later, Crazy Horse came across Black Buffalo Woman gathering herbs and plants as he returned from a hunting party. Ashamed, Black Buffalo Woman threw her blanket over her head. When Crazy Horse rode up beside her, she removed the blanket and told him she had followed the wishes of her family. "I had my duty to my father and brothers," she said. Crazy Horse told Black Buffalo Woman that while he loved her, he could accept her marriage. "I would have everything good between us," Crazy Horse said. "I have made a vow that it should be so. There can be no anger in my heart, even against myself."[9]

Crazy Horse rode off, leaving Black Buffalo Woman alone with the painful realization that she had married the wrong man. But all was not over between the young Oglala warrior and the woman who had captured his heart.

The second significant event took place in the summer of 1865, when seven Oglala leaders who were over forty met to discuss tribal governance. These tribal leaders, called "the Big Bellies," were selected to advise and govern the Oglala in important tribal matters such as moving the camp, hunting, and making war. The question of war, as troubles with the whites grew, was much on the minds of the Sioux. Traditionally, the Big Bellies selected four younger men and called them "Shirt-Wearers." These arrangements were made to carry out their edicts in an informal fashion, without anything like an election by the people. The Sioux had a great deal of trust in the wisdom and leadership of their elders. As a result, the actual responsibilities and duties of the Shirt-Wearers were unclear.

Nevertheless, the ceremony to install the Shirt-Wearers was important to the Oglalas, who were camped that summer on a creek about seventy miles from Fort Laramie. Warriors and chiefs on horseback, dressed in battle regalia, formed a circle inside a ring of chanting women and children, who stood in front of their lodges. Each time the warriors made a circuit, they selected a young warrior and led him to the center of the camp. The first three braves selected were Young-Man-Afraid-of-Horses; Sword, the son of a powerful chief; and American Horse. All came from prominent Oglala families. It was, therefore, a surprise when the mounted warriors passed by the sons of other prominent fathers and selected Crazy Horse as their final choice. Crazy Horse's father was no chief and his family, while respected, was not known for great wealth or status.

The Big Bellies then selected a wise old man to speak for the tribe. The Shirt-Wearers, the old man said, would now head the warriors in the camp. They would see that law and order were preserved; they were to be given extraordinary powers. In certain cases, the Shirt-Wearers had the power of life and death over members of the tribe. Thus, he said, it was essential for them to be wise, kind, and just.

A sheepskin shirt was given to each of the four young men. The shirts were fringed with hair and each lock of hair represented a deed of courage and bravery. The shirt of Crazy Horse had over 240 locks of hair.

Another senior Oglala addressed the Shirt-Wearers. He told them that they had been chosen for their strength of character and that they must, therefore, never think of themselves. He said,

> Wear the shirts, my sons, and be big-hearted men, always helping others, never thinking of yourselves. Look out for the poor, the widows and orphans and all those of little power; help them. Think no ill of others, nor see the ill they would do you. . . . Do not give way to anger, even if relatives lie in blood before you. I know these things are hard to do, my sons, but we have chosen you as great-hearted. Do all these duties gladly, and with a good face. Be generous and strong and brave in them, and if for all these things an enemy comes against you, go boldly forward, for it is better to lie a naked warrior in death than to be wrapped up well with a heart of water inside.[10]

In the following years, Crazy Horse gained renown as an Oglala Shirt-Wearer. Meanwhile, relations between the Plains tribes and the whites worsened even while the American Civil War raged in the east. The problem whites faced on the plains during the 1860s were compounded by the Civil War. Most available troops and the best military officers had been thrown into the war between the states. The units on the plains were, with a few exceptions, the dregs of the American military, and their commanders were often worse, since frontier service was considered unimportant. Thus, at a time when whites were streaming into Sioux territory, there was little American military might around to protect them. Along with the honest homesteaders, there were draft dodgers, army deserters, gamblers, soldiers of fortune, prospectors, and fools—anyone who wanted to avoid the Civil War. All were heading west in these years, along the Oregon Trail. For many of the younger Sioux warriors, including Crazy Horse, attacking the white settlers was easier than going out on dangerous war parties against the Crows or Pawnees. And the rewards were greater. Although Crazy Horse and others joined with Sioux bands in attacking whites, the Oglalas, for the most part, simply avoided them. As Stephen E. Ambrose observed,

> While the other Indians were fighting the whites to the north, west, south, and east of the Powder River, the Oglala Sioux continued until 1865 to act as if they had solved the problem of white encroachment for all time by the simple expedient of moving out of the way of the whites.[11]

There were exceptions to the typical mediocrity of the officers sent out to the frontier in these years. Lieutenant Caspar Collins, the son of the commander of Fort Laramie, Colonel William O. Collins, did his best to understand the Sioux. Young Collins became a respected friend to the Indians. He often traveled by himself through Sioux territory and stayed with the various Sioux bands. In the winter of 1863–64, Collins spent time with the Oglalas. Crazy Horse got to know the young white officer and liked him. Together the two young warriors from different cultures went off on hunting trips where Crazy Horse would show Collins how to make a bow and arrows. Crazy Horse even instructed Collins in the Dakota language.[12]

But men like Collins were exceptions. Far more typical was Colonel John M. Chivington, who was commissioned as an officer during the Civil War. Chivington, an elder in the Methodist Church, was a large man, over six feet tall, and he weighed around 250 pounds. A native of Ohio, Chivington preached his way west, eventually settling in Denver, Colorado. As a minister who often preached to the rough-and-tumble frontiersmen and miners in the saloons and mining camps, Chivington was no stranger to violence. In fact, he liked it.

It was said that Chivington wanted to go into politics, and the best way to get votes on the western frontier in these troubled years was to present yourself as a fearless Indian fighter, known for going up against "the bloodthirsty redskins." All the eager Chivington needed to swing his troops into action was an incident. With white–Indian relations under strain all over the western frontier, it wasn't long before Chivington had one.

On June 11, 1864, a family of settlers living twenty miles east of Denver were murdered and scalped, their ranch burned, and their livestock stolen. The crime was committed by four young Arapaho. When the mutilated victims were brought to Denver and displayed, John Evans, the governor of Colorado territory, worried that all-out war would break out in his region. Evans issued a proclamation calling on all the plains tribes in his area to report to certain forts, to avoid "being killed by mistake" by angry whites.[13]

To compound matters, Colonel Chivington had received a report that some government cattle had been stolen. That was enough for Chivington, who called his Third Colorado Volunteer Regiment into action. It did not matter to Chivington which Indians had stolen the cattle, or even if any cattle had actually been stolen.[14]

Although the Cheyenne were among the fiercest tribes on the plains, a number of their chiefs wanted no part of a conflict they did not start. One Cheyenne band, led by Chief Black Kettle, came into Fort Lyon for a meeting with Governor Evans, Chivington, and other Colorado authorities. To show their good faith the Cheyenne turned over four white children who had been taken as captives, and the chiefs promised to give up three other children as soon as they could be brought in from other Cheyenne villages. It should have been clear to the Colorado authorities that although some of their younger braves might have been involved in hostile activities, the Cheyenne wanted peace and their leaders were people of honor.

At the meeting Black Kettle spoke frankly: "All we ask is that we may have peace with the whites," he said. To impress the chiefs, Governor Evans told the Cheyenne that many white soldiers would be coming into the territory now that the American Civil War was over. At the same time, Black Kettle was led to believe that if he brought his people in, they would be under the governor's protection. The last to speak at the meeting was Colonel Chivington, who told the Indians, "I am not a big war chief, but all the soldiers in this country are at my command. My rule of fighting white men or Indians is to fight them until they lay down their arms and submit."[15]

The Cheyenne chiefs left the meeting content the authorities had accepted their peace overtures. Black Kettle did as he was advised and moved his band to Sand Creek, about forty miles from Fort Lyon. To show his good faith, the Cheyenne chief ran up an American flag in the center of his village. But in August of 1864 Governor Evans, to play it safe, had issued a proclamation urging all white citizens to arm themselves, form parties to hunt down hostile Indians, and kill every hostile they might come across. Once again, no distinctions were made between the Indians. An Indian was an Indian, as armed bands of whites roamed the territory shooting them on sight. The Indians, in retaliation, formed war parties and killed whites. At the center of this sorry mess was Colonel John M. Chivington.[16]

Chivington's Third Colorado Volunteers was a force of

about 750 men including all the Indian-haters Chivington could muster in Denver: gamblers, drunks, and gunfighters who had volunteered for one hundred days to kill Indians. Chivington was determined that "his boys" have some action before their enlistment was up. On November 28, they arrived at Fort Lyon ready for a fight.

Chivington made it clear to the fort's commander, Major Scott Anthony, that he was going to attack the Cheyenne at Sand Creek. Although a number of junior officers protested that the Cheyenne had come to Sand Creek under the protection of the Colorado authorities, Chivington became abusive. Lieutenant Joseph Cramer later testified that Chivington "believed it to be right and honorable to use any means under God's heaven to kill Indians that would kill women and children and 'damn any man that was in sympathy with the Indians.'" That evening Chivington rode out from Fort Lyon at the head of his regiment. The troop rode all night, arriving at Sand Creek early on the morning of November 29. Chivington gave his men firm instructions: "Kill and scalp all, big and little; nits make lice."[17]

Chivington's force attacked at dawn, after he had sent out a detachment to run off the Cheyenne herd of some five hundred ponies. Chivington was not about to allow a single Cheyenne to escape. As dawn broke, a Cheyenne woman coming out of her lodge saw the soldiers in the hills overlooking the camp. She shouted the alarm but it was too late. The army's cannons were already in place and immediately opened up on the sleeping camp.

Black Kettle, in a futile gesture, ran the United States flag and a white flag up the pole. He was dragged away and saved by some young braves, although his wife was shot seven times. The Cheyenne village erupted in chaos as people ran in all directions to escape the exploding cannon shot and the charging cavalrymen. Younger warriors were immediately overwhelmed as they ran out of their lodges without their weapons.

White Antelope, a Cheyenne chief well over seventy,

refused to retreat. He folded his arms, stood his ground, and stared at the advancing whites as he chanted his death song: "Nothing lives long, except the earth and the mountains." A bullet cut him down. George Bent, a half-Cheyenne who had been forced to accompany Chivington as a scout from Fort Lyon, was devastated by the scene:

> I saw five squaws under a bank. When troops came up to them they ran out and showed their persons to let the soldiers know they were squaws and begged for mercy but the soldiers shot them all. I saw one squaw on a bank whose leg had been broken by a shell. A soldier came up to her with drawn saber. She raised her arm to protect herself when he struck, breaking her arm; she rolled over and raised her other arm when he struck, breaking it.... Some thirty or forty squaws ... sent out a little girl about six years old with a white flag on a stick. She was shot and killed.... I saw one squaw cut open with an unborn child lying by her side. I saw the body of White Antelope with the privates cut off, and I heard a soldier say he was going to make a tobacco pouch out of them....[18]

Still, the Cheyenne regrouped and fought bravely. Major Anthony later said, "I never saw more bravery displayed by any set of people on the face of the earth than by these Indians. They would charge on the whole company singly, determined to kill someone before being killed themselves."[19]

The massacre at Sand Creek lasted for hours and went on into the afternoon, with soldiers mercilessly cutting down escaping Cheyenne women and children. When it was over, some 270 Cheyenne and 40 visiting Arapahos had been killed. Among them were 200 women and children. George Bent, the half-Cheyenne from Fort Lyon, fought the Indians and was wounded. He stayed in the camp to count the dead. His estimate was that 163 were killed, and of those, 110 were women and children. Whatever the actual figure, the massacre at Sand Creek is one of the most brutal episodes in the history of the American West.

Colonel Chivington, in addition to being a boastful coward, was also a liar. In his report he wrote, "I at daylight this morning attacked a Cheyenne village of . . . from nine hundred to a thousand warriors. We killed . . . between four and five hundred. All did nobly." In between acts of a Denver theatrical performance, the scalps of the mutilated Cheyenne women were displayed for the audience. The *Denver News* praised Chivington and "his boys" as great frontier heroes, writing, "All acquitted themselves well. Colorado soldiers have again covered themselves with glory."

But not everyone saw Chivington and his men as heroes. There was widespread condemnation of his actions in the eastern press and among humanitarian groups. A military commission investigated and called thirty-three witnesses; seventeen condemned Chivington, who was forced to resign his commission under threat of a court-martial. The frontier scout Kit Carson, well known as a fearless Indian fighter, testified as an expert witness. He called Chivington and "his boys" cowards and dogs. Eventually, Congress made the small gesture of giving reparations to the few women and children who had survived Sand Creek.[20]

Some scholars believe that Chivington helped unite the Plains Indians against the Americans. By killing friendly Indians, Chivington sent a message to the western tribes and converted the Cheyenne and Arapaho survivors into furious enemies, determined to avenge the terrible wrongs committed at Sand Creek.[21]

Word of Sand Creek filtered slowly across the plains. The Cheyennes who escaped called for all-out war (though Black Kettle himself still wanted peace). When word reached the Oglalas, there was great mourning. Many of the Oglalas had friends and relatives killed at Sand Creek. The Oglalas were particularly angry when they heard that

Cheyenne women had been cut open and mutilated. They listened in shock as they were told how Cheyenne scalps had been displayed in saloons in Denver. Crazy Horse was especially affected. Among those killed was Yellow Woman, the Cheyenne he had saved after the Harney massacre.

When the runners who brought the news of Sand Creek finished speaking, Crazy Horse walked out into the snowy hills. What could it mean? Crazy Horse looked for a sign. He saw a spotted eagle soaring high overhead and then swooping low. Then he saw a broken feather drifting slowly down to earth.

Crazy Horse thought carefully about the ten years since Conquering Bear had died. All the treaties, all the efforts to avoid the whites, all of the supposed peace had come to nothing for the Indian. The frontier was going up in flames. Spotted Tail's Brulés and many Oglalas would rally to the side of their Cheyenne brothers to fight the whites. It was not what Crazy Horse wanted, even though he had little love for the whites. But he was an Oglala leader—a Shirt-Wearer. There were many other young warriors like him who would feel the same way. It would be war.[22]

Within days, Sioux, Cheyenne, and Arapaho raiding parties roamed the plains, striking wherever whites had settled. Ranches, trading posts, and wagon trains along the Oregon Trail were no longer safe. As one scholar noted, "Indians, driving their freshly captured livestock and with their horses loaded with plunder, moved across the plains in the direction of the Black Hills. Behind them they left ravaged settlements, burned buildings, and the corpses of many Americans. The white men had paid a heavy price for Colonel Chivington's attack on Black Kettle and the friendly Cheyennes."[23]

C RAZY H ORSE
AND THE B ATTLE OF
A H UNDRED S LAIN

Give me eighty men and I would ride through the whole Sioux nation.
—Captain William J. Fetterman (1866)

In early 1865, for a brief time, the Indians seemed in control and had the plains to themselves. With the Platte River region terrorized and the soldiers ineffectual against the Sioux, the tribes continued to raid and plunder. The army officers stationed in the area tried to distance themselves from blame for the Sioux triumphs and stay out of their way.

That winter the Sioux moved entire villages as they took to the warpath. One observer wrote,

> *These Indians had moved four hundred miles during the worst weather of a severe winter through open, desolate plains taking with them their women and children, lodges and household property, their vast herds of ponies, and the herds of captured cattle, horses and mules. On the way they had killed more whites than the number of Cheyennes killed at Sand Creek and had completely destroyed one hundred miles of the Overland Stage Line.[1]*

But the forces of history were moving against the Sioux and their allies. Although a few Sioux living around the forts had some idea of the military might the whites could ultimately bring against their people, the more warlike Sioux despised those Indians they disparagingly called "Loafers" or "Hang-Around-the-Forts." Over the years these Indians had become lazy and dependent on the handouts of the whites at Fort Laramie. Many Loafers had heard tales of a fierce three-day battle at a place called Gettysburg. If the stories they heard were true, the real power of the white soldiers had not yet been seen.

The soldiers at Fort Laramie angered many of the local Sioux by hanging two Oglala chiefs who, to show their peaceful intentions, had brought in a captive white woman. The woman claimed that she had been molested. The temporary commander of the fort, drunk at the time, ordered the two men hanged without questioning why men guilty of rape would bring their victim to the fort to testify against them. Thus, instead of encouraging the friendly Sioux to work with them as scouts, the army alienated many of the "friendlies," who began feeding information on troop movements to the "hostiles."[2]

By the spring of 1865, the Civil War was drawing to a close. Troops now free from service in the east, along with a new and eager command staff, were rushed out to the plains to deal with the rampaging Indians. Throughout early 1865 the Sioux and their allies had been sending small raiding parties against the whites. Crazy Horse led many of these war parties as he and other Oglala leaders watched the buildup of United States Army strength along the frontier. The Sioux attacked every wagon train coming up the Platte River, and such warriors as Crazy Horse, Hump, and Young-Man-Afraid-of-Horses led the war parties that ranged as far south as Fort Reno on the Dry Fork River, and even, sometimes, to Fort Laramie itself. Crazy Horse and his braves often joined Red Cloud's warriors in the hills overlooking the fort, where they watched the comings and goings with binoculars and sent smoke signals to let the other hostile bands of Sioux know what the soldiers were doing.[3]

One new officer, Major General G. M. Dodge, who had taken command of the military Department of the Missouri, stupidly ordered that all friendly Indians around Fort Laramie either be attacked or removed to Fort Kearney in Nebraska, on the lower Platte River. This forced march of about fifteen hundred friendly Loafers and Brulés, still led by Spotted Tail, put the Indians in great danger. Most had been disarmed by the soldiers, and they would be moving through the territory of their bitter enemies, the Pawnee.

But Dodge was adamant and on June 11, 1865, over a thousand friendly Sioux started to march southeast, guarded by a small force of 135 men from the Seventh Iowa Cavalry. As they traveled, the soldiers abused the Indians and often brutalized them. They threw youngsters into the Platte, swollen by heavy spring rains, and molested young Sioux women. What the soldiers did not know was that an Oglala war party led by Crazy Horse was tracking them.

On the night of June 13, Crazy Horse crept into the camp of his captive kinspeople and met with their leaders. He told them that he had enough warriors across the river to protect them if they wanted to make a break for freedom. Spotted Tail and the other leaders agreed, and Crazy Horse left to prepare his warriors to defend the escaping captives against any pursuit.

The next day, June 14, 1865, the captive Sioux refused to pack up their camp and an angry army captain rode into their midst, shouting. He cursed the Indians and ordered them to get moving. A warrior killed him as the remaining soldiers, realizing that they were greatly outnumbered, fled. The Sioux gathered up their things and raced for the North Platte, where Crazy Horse waited with his Oglalas. Over a thousand Sioux escaped and scattered north, where they soon joined up with other hostiles. In the meantime, Crazy Horse and Spotted Tail joined forces to drive the fleeing soldiers back across the Platte.

Crazy Horse was just twenty-four at this time,

although he was already a famous warrior among the Oglalas. He was not a very big man, no more than 5 feet 7 or 8 inches in height and weighing only around 140 pounds. Although not as fair as he had been as a child, his hair and skin were lighter than those of other Sioux. His hair fell below his waist and was generally tied in braids. In battle, he usually wore only a breechcloth and leggings although, on occasion, he wore a white buckskin shirt. White Bull, a close friend, reported that Crazy Horse always painted his face with white spots before a fight. When he went into battle he threw a handful of earth over himself and his horse. He wore a single hawk feather in his hair instead of the many-feathered warbonnet of other war chiefs. He carried a small stone that he wedged behind his ear and another stone, a gift from his good friend Chips, an Oglala medicine man, tied under his left arm. He was an imposing figure on the battlefield.[4]

For the first time since the early 1840s, the Sioux were making a concerted effort to defend their sacred lands and drive the whites from the plains. Over one thousand lodges supplied braves dressed in battle regalia to go against the whites along the Holy Road. In addition to the Oglalas and Cheyenne there were Minniconjou, Brulés (though Spotted Tail didn't seem to support this expedition), Sans Arcs, Loafers (Hang-Around-the-Forts), and Arapaho.

According to George Bent (the half-Cheyenne who now rode with the Indians), the leaders of this massive war party were a Northern Cheyenne, Roman Nose, and the Oglalas, Young-Man-Afraid-of-Horses and Red Cloud. The Oglalas even established a line of communication with Sitting Bull, who led the far northern Hunkpapas in the Montana country and North Dakota. Sitting Bull, who had always opposed accepting annuities from the whites and viewed them as the enemy, led a force of four hundred Sioux against the soldiers at Fort Rice on the Missouri River in North Dakota. At the same time, the Oglalas and Cheyenne were attacking in force along the Oregon Trail.

Even with their massive numbers, the Indians lost a

Sitting Bull surrounded by his mother, two sisters, daughter, and grandson.

military advantage and made a serious tactical error. Without a solid line of communications, the Sioux did not know that the whites were vulnerable. The military outposts were not yet fully manned, and since the combined forces of the Oglalas and Cheyenne alone numbered three thousand warriors, the Indians had the upper hand. But they did not act. And this was their last opportunity to overwhelm the white forces, who were now ready to turn their attention to the difficulties on the plains. As historian Stephen E. Ambrose writes,

> The Oglalas should have gone farther east, at least to Fort Laramie and even better to Fort Kearney in central Nebraska, while Sitting Bull should have attacked farther south, at Fort Sully or Fort Randall in South Dakota. A successful assault on Forts Sully and Kearney, followed by a determined effort to hold both places, would have isolated the forts upstream on the Missouri and the Platte. Forts Laramie and Rice would have quickly fallen of their own weight without a steady flow of supplies.[5]

There were many skirmishes and a few minor battles between the Sioux and the white soldiers in what became known as the Powder River War. In the end little was accomplished, although the Indians outnumbered the white troops on the plains by a hundred to one or even more. Over three thousand Sioux and Cheyenne warriors had spent weeks preparing for war. After a three-day march the Indians had killed only eight whites. Part of the problem may have been that the soldiers outgunned the Indians. One estimate is that for every hundred braves, the Oglalas had but one gun. Whatever the reason, the war changed little in the balance of power on the expanding frontier. Time was on the side of the whites and against the Sioux and other Plains Indians.[6]

Four years after Colonel Chivington's victory over the Cheyenne at Sand Creek, a United States government commission reported on the war that followed: "It scarcely has its parallel in the records of Indian barbarity. . . . No one will be astonished that a war ensued which cost the government $30,000,000 and carried conflagration and death to the border settlements. . . ."[7]

By late summer of 1865, over two thousand soldiers were sent to Fort Laramie. They immediately set out for the Powder River country where the Oglalas, led by Red Cloud and Crazy Horse, had been rampaging. The objective was clear: to teach the Sioux and Cheyenne a lesson and force them onto a reservation either along the Missouri River or, if possible, in Oklahoma. The discovery of gold in Montana made it necessary for the whites to cut a new trail running north. Thus, the soldiers wanted to provide safe passage along this new road, the Bozeman Trail, to be cut from the Oregon Trail west of Fort Laramie, directly northwest to Montana and the gold mines. Red Cloud and his Oglalas were in the way.

The men in these regiments had just come from combat in the Civil War. They had little interest in fighting Indians and wanted only to get out of the army as quickly as possible. The Sioux played hit-and-run with these forces, running off with their horses and making their lives miserable. Many soldiers deserted, and some mutinied. When the troops finally arrived back at Fort Laramie, they were in terrible condition.[8]

Meanwhile, in Washington, under pressure from Quakers and other humanitarian groups, the American government was about to formulate a new policy for the Indians of the western frontier. With the radical Republicans in control of the Congress, there was great pressure on the government to live up to the promise of equality for all minorities, including the Indians. Drained emotionally and financially by four years of fierce civil war, the government decided that the problems of the Great Plains could not be solved militarily. It was decided to buy the Indians off with a new treaty and another annuity. The commander for the upper Missouri, General John Pope, objected. Writing to secretary of the interior, James Harlan, Pope said, "The

Indians now in hostility need some exhibition of force, and some punishment before they will be peaceful. . . . The treaty of peace . . . is, I presume, such a treaty as it has been the practice of the Indian Department to make heretofore . . . paying Indians for outrages committed upon innocent women and children."[9]

Nevertheless, in the fall of 1865 a treaty council met at Fort Sully on the banks of the Missouri River. The years of fighting had interrupted the buffalo hunts and trade. Thus, deprived of the guns, ammunition, and other goods they had been receiving from the whites, some Sioux bands had serious problems. Hundreds of starving eastern Sioux responded to the call for peace and rode in to meet with the government agents.

By the end of October 1865, the American agents claimed to have concluded treaties with nine Sioux bands, including the seven Teton groups. These treaties were similar, with the Indians agreeing to keep peace and to stop attacking the settlers traveling the Oregon and Bozeman trails. In exchange, the United States agreed to pay the bands a collective annuity of $76,900 a year for twenty years. Once again the American government miscalculated and once again American officials demonstrated an appalling ignorance of Sioux life and culture.

Although the Indian commissioners reported that the chiefs signing these agreements represented over ten thousand Sioux, they also knew that there were twenty thousand hostile Sioux camped in the Powder River and Black Hills country who were not in favor of these new treaties. Thus, even though the commissioners claimed these treaties were concluded with "the Sioux Nation," only two months later a band of Red Cloud's Oglalas attacked a government surveying party, stripping them of their clothes and gear before releasing them naked into the northwest. The treaty was broken and shown to be useless even before it reached lawmakers in Washington.[10]

And so the United States government embarked on a two-tier policy toward the Indians of the Plains. On one level, sympathetic Indian agents were sent out by the Department of Interior to meet with Indian leaders in order to make peace. On another level, some of the best military men in the United States Army were dispatched to bring order to the western frontier and pave the way for the expansion of the nation.

As the new railroad tracks began to open a way west in 1866, Major General William Tecumseh Sherman was put in command of the Missouri District (the Department of the Mississippi), a vast territory that stretched from the Mississippi River all the way west to the Rocky Mountains. General Sherman, a Union hero of the Civil War who brought a war of destruction to the very heart of the South, was assigned the responsibility of protecting the Bozeman Trail and the railroads. Writing to his superior, General Ulysses S. Grant, in the spring of 1866, Sherman said, "[I]t is our duty to . . . make the progress of construction of the great Pacific railways . . . as safe as possible."[11]

William Tecumseh Sherman, despite his middle name, had little concern for the Indians who stood in the way of American progress and Manifest Destiny. In 1867 he said,

> The more [Indians] we can kill this year, the less will have to be killed the next war, for the more I see of these Indians, the more convinced I am that they all have to be killed or be maintained as a species of paupers.[12]

Sherman immediately dispatched Colonel Henry Carrington and a battalion of infantry to give "the best possible protection to . . . the region of Montana and the routes thereto." Carrington set out for Fort Laramie at the head of the Bozeman Trail. He was intent on constructing two forts in the vicinity of the Sioux's Powder River hunting grounds no matter what were the results of the peace efforts with the hostiles.

Still, the agents for peace on the plains proceeded. In June 1866, the federal government's principal negotiator, E. B. Taylor, met with Red Cloud and other prominent Oglala

97

and Brulé leaders after promising them gifts if they would come in to Fort Laramie. Crazy Horse and many of the younger warriors wanted no part of such a meeting. They had taken plenty of goods in raids and had no need of the whites' gifts. But Red Cloud and Young-Man-Afraid-of-Horses believed it wouldn't hurt to see what was being offered for peace. Besides, there was the possibility of getting arms and ammunition, which were always in short supply.

Taylor argued for peace and dwelt on the large annuity. He promised arms and ammunition, but he never mentioned the two forts that were to be built in the Powder River country. In the midst of these talks, Colonel Carrington's men marched into Fort Laramie. Red Cloud was a canny politician who knew the whites; nor were the other Oglala chiefs naive. They all understood what a large force of bluecoats meant. They saw through the government's two-faced policy of seeking peace, while at the same time reinforcing the garrison along the very road under dispute.

Red Cloud was furious. He picked up his blanket and, pointing at Carrington's newly arrived battalion, denounced the peace: "The Great Father sends us presents and wants us to sell him the road, but White Chief goes with soldiers to steal the road before the Indians say Yes or No." Then he stormed out of the meeting. Arriving back at his Powder River camp, Red Cloud spoke to his people:

> Hear ye Dakotas ... the Great Father is building his forts among us. You have heard the sound of the white soldiers' axe upon the Little Piney. His presence here is an insult to the spirits of our ancestors. Are we to give up their sacred grounds to be plowed for corn? I am for war.[13]

Although Crazy Horse's uncle, the Brulé chief Spotted Tail, and some older chiefs signed Taylor's treaty, it meant little. Spotted Tail had spent a year in prison at Fort Leavenworth and was convinced the Sioux could not overcome the whites' vast numbers and military strength. A few signatures from some old peace chiefs would not protect the Bozeman Trail from attack by Sioux still hostile to white intrusion.[14]

Taylor sent a message to Washington: "Satisfactory treaty concluded with the Sioux . . . most cordial feeling prevails." He barely mentioned Red Cloud, noting that he was an unimportant leader of a small band of insurgents. The government believed peace had finally come to the plains. President Andrew Johnson told the American people that the Sioux had "unconditionally submitted to our authority and manifested an earnest desire for a renewal of friendly relations."[15]

The soldiers and officers on the frontier knew better. By August of 1866 Carrington had marched to Piney Creek about halfway between the Powder and Bighorn rivers. There he constructed the new post, Fort Phil Kearny. Carrington then split his forces, sending two companies north to set up Fort C. F. Smith on the Bighorn River. (Both forts were named for Union officers in the Civil War.) That left Carrington with only 350 troops to protect a hundred miles of the Bozeman Trail against thousands of hostile Sioux.[16]

Only two days after Fort Kearny was built, the Sioux attacked, killing two soldiers and wounding three while making off with 175 horses and mules. Up and down the Bozeman, between Forts Reno and Kearny, Red Cloud and his military genius, Crazy Horse, led the Sioux to make life miserable for the soldiers and white settlers.

The Sioux were so determined to stop the white incursion into their lands that Red Cloud even arranged a truce with their traditional enemies, the Crows, so that every available warrior and all their resources could be used against the whites.[17] Red Cloud and Crazy Horse were convinced that the Sioux were now in a final struggle for control of the Powder River region. The Sioux were fighting for their survival and for their way of life.

Red Cloud was the politician and Crazy Horse was the tactician—the military brains. Red Cloud traveled throughout the Great Plains, rallying the various tribes to his banner—Oglalas, Minniconjous, Hunkpapas, Sans Arcs, Brulés, and northern Cheyenne and Arapaho. Like Tecumseh before him, Red Cloud urged them to put aside their ancient tribal differences and join in a common war against the whites.

For months, from August to December 1866, the Indians harassed Fort Kearny, killing soldiers and travelers while stealing horses, cattle, and mules. Life inside the fort became difficult and oppressive for the soldiers and the women who had traveled west with their husbands. They ventured outside the fort at great risk. Not a single wagon train came up the Bozeman Trail unmolested during this time. Colonel Carrington was disturbed by settlers who paid little heed to the military's warnings about the danger of travel in the region. Finally, he declared that to travel the Bozeman, a wagon train had to have at least forty able-bodied men. But even that did little good. The wagon trains rolled and the Indians attacked in the hit-and-run guerilla style that Crazy Horse and his warriors practiced.[18]

Many of the Fort Kearny officers were unhappy with Colonel Carrington's conservative stay-in-the-fort response to the Indians. They were ambitious and hungry for action against the Indians, who they scorned as undisciplined fighters. One malcontent was Captain William J. Fetterman, Carrington's second-in-command. Fetterman was contemptuous of his commander and of the fighting ability of the Sioux. Fetterman was typical of the arrogant officers the War Department regularly dispatched to the western frontier. He was often heard bragging, "Give me eighty men and I would ride through the whole Sioux nation." Fetterman was determined to advance his military career over the dead bodies of as many Sioux as he could find and kill. Ultimately, he found more fight than he bargained for when, by December 1866, Red Cloud assembled over a thousand warriors across a forty-mile range in the Powder River region.

The Indians outnumbered the soldiers by at least six to

one, yet Crazy Horse knew that he had to draw Carrington's men out of Fort Kearny in order to engage them. With only a few guns, the Indians were short of firepower, while all the soldiers carried single-shot rifles. In the open, however, the Sioux and their allies could overwhelm them.

On December 6, Crazy Horse and Red Cloud led about three hundred warriors and another smaller force in an effort to lure the soldiers into a trap. It was early winter, with snow already on the ground, and Kearny was in desperate need of firewood. Colonel Carrington sent out a wagon party to chop and gather wood, with Captain Fetterman and forty cavalry along to protect them.

Red Cloud signaled a hundred decoys to attack the wood train. As Red Cloud had hoped, Fetterman and his men turned to pursue the attackers, who rode off. But the Indian plan to draw Fetterman into an ambush didn't work when Carrington rode up with forty soldiers and, after some fierce fighting, ordered a retreat.

The combined units returned to the fort. Fetterman was outraged at Carrington for ordering a retreat. After a Sioux attack on a wagon train on December 19, when Carrington again ordered no pursuit, Fetterman vowed that the next time there would be no retreat—he would head an offensive and engage the Sioux. Fetterman asked his commander for permission to lead one hundred soldiers to attack the entire Indian camp along the Tongue River. Carrington refused, but he may have been tempted to allow the foolish braggart to take on four thousand of Red Cloud's warriors.[19]

On December 21, 1866, Fetterman finally got his chance for action. The last logging party of the season had gone out from Fort Kearny and sent back word that it was under attack. Fetterman convinced Carrington to give him command of the relief unit. Although Carrington was suspicious, he gave Fetterman the command along with written and verbal orders: "Support the wood train. Relieve it and report to me. Do not engage or pursue Indians at its expense. Under not circumstances pursue over the ridge. . . ."

Fetterman was joined by Captain Frederick H. Brown, who was to be transferred in a few days. Brown begged for "one more chance to bring in the scalp of Red Cloud myself." In a twist of historical irony—Fetterman had stated he could defeat the entire Sioux Nation with eighty men—Fetterman left Fort Kearny in command of eighty men.[20]

One historian of the Indian wars, writing in 1886, was baffled. He noted that as Fetterman left the fort and reached Lodge Trail Ridge just before noon, the attacking Indians disappeared. Then Fetterman and his force halted briefly on the crest of the ridge and "disappeared over the summit. . . . Just what happened after Fetterman's command passed the top of Lodge Ridge no one can say, for no man lived to tell it." The historian, whose sympathies were with the whites, never interviewed any Sioux or Cheyenne.[21]

What happened that day demonstrated the tactical skill of Crazy Horse. As Fetterman and his troops rode out of Fort Kearny, the Sioux decoys were led out of hiding by Crazy Horse. Fetterman approached the besieged wood wagons, and Crazy Horse and his decoy warriors first appeared to charge and then, seeing Fetterman's large force, rode off whooping and shouting as if terrified. At the same time, after an order from Red Cloud, Hump signaled the contingent of Indians attacking the wagons to retreat toward Lodge Trail Ridge as if they, too, were afraid. The ruse worked on Fetterman.[22]

Now it was Crazy Horse's show and he, like the other decoys, pretended at first to mock the soldiers. Fetterman discarded Carrington's cautionary orders and stared down the slope as Crazy Horse and the other decoys jumped up and down jeering and waving their blankets at the soldiers. At that moment, the Indians retreating from the attack on the wood wagon joined Crazy Horse and, seeing Fetterman's troops, galloped off. With one hand Crazy Horse, in the rear, beat his pony to a hard gallop, in full view of Fetterman and his troops. But with his unseen other hand he reined in the horse so it would not get too far away. The taunts and the opportunity to kill Indians was a combination Fetterman was unable to resist, and so he gave the order to pursue. His troops disappeared over the crest and down the Bozeman trail, chasing the retreating Indians.[23]

Fetterman believed he had the Indians on the run. He was convinced that when he caught up with the retreating and cowardly Indians, he would simply crush them. Crazy Horse managed to stay just out of reach, using one ruse after another. Once he jumped off his pony to examine its foot as if it had gone lame. He appeared frustrated, throwing up his hands in despair. At the last moment he jumped back on the pony and galloped off, keeping the pursuing troops at a safe distance. At another point, afraid that the soldiers might give up the chase because they were too far behind, Crazy Horse stopped to build a small fire and did not get moving again until the soldiers' bullets began to splatter in the snow around him.[24] Then Crazy Horse acted fatigued and ready to surrender. At the last moment, he rode off. He kept up this game until he approached the top of Lodge Trail Ridge, about five miles from the fort.

The excited Fetterman was still urging his men forward. They chased Crazy Horse to the top of the ridge and down into the valley toward Peno Creek. Once in that valley the trap was sprung. Some two thousand Sioux, Cheyenne, and Arapaho came charging out from all flanks. Fetterman wheeled his horse, looking back at the direction from which he had come. But there was no chance of retreat or escape. Shouting chilling war cries, Indians were coming at him and his men from every direction.

The infantrymen were all killed as the Indians fell upon them in fierce hand-to-hand combat. Fetterman and his cavalry dismounted, turned their horses loose, and retreated to some rocks on a hill near the end of the ridge to put up a last ditch fight.[25]

The battle lasted about forty minutes. Arrows rained down from every direction as the soldiers searched for any place to get away from the fierce onslaught. One historian estimates that the Indians fired as many as forty thousand

Crazy Horse's first victory against the U.S. Army was on December 21, 1866, when he and his warriors wiped out Captain William J. Fetterman and eighty cavalrymen in the Battle of the Hundred Slain.

arrows that day. Only four soldiers were hit by bullets. When the battle was over, Fetterman and his eighty men lay dead. At the last minute, rather than be taken captive, Captains Fetterman and Brown placed their pistols against each other's heads, counted to three, and fired. The Fetterman Massacre, or the Battle of the Hundred Slain, as the Indians called it, was over.[26]

The Indians then charged in and, with Sand Creek still fresh in their minds, mutilated the bodies. Historian

Stephen E. Ambrose says that, "Cutting up the soldiers' bodies helped the Indians relieve their tension and made the victory more satisfying and complete. It was not a typical Indian action."[27]

Colonel Carrington was appalled by what he found. But as another scholar, Dee Brown, has written,

> Had Colonel Carrington visited the scene of the Sand Creek Massacre ... he would have seen the same mutilations—committed upon Indians by Colonel Chivington's soldiers. The Indians who ambushed Fetterman were only imitating their enemies, a practice which in warfare, as in civilian life, is said to be the sincerest form of flattery.[28]

Carrington wrote a report pleading for reinforcements and dispatched a civilian volunteer, the famous scout John "Portugee" Phillips, to ride with news of the Fetterman Massacre to Fort Laramie, 236 miles away. Phillips bravely rode through the surrounding Indians and a raging snowstorm on Carrington's own thoroughbred horse, arriving at Fort Laramie four days later. Meanwhile, Carrington prepared for an all-out attack on his post. But the attack never came because the Indians, including Crazy Horse, were content with what they had achieved and didn't want to fight in the bad weather. The Sioux left the area to seek shelter without striking what could have been the final blow against the soldiers.[29]

Repercussions from the Fetterman Massacre were immediate. The western press accused the army of cowardice for not wiping out the Indians. The *Montana Post* editorialized, "If the Indians continue their barbarities, wipe them out." The *Kansas Daily Tribune* stated: "There can be no permanent, lasting peace on the frontier till these devils are exterminated."[30]

Genocidal words like *extermination* were not confined to the western press. They began appearing in the public statements of military leaders of the day. General William

Tecumseh Sherman, who had minimized the dangers ahead for Carrington and his troops out on the Bozeman Trail, said,

> I do not understand how the massacre of Colonel [sic] Fetterman's party could have been so complete. . . . We must act with vindictive earnestness against the Sioux, even to their extermination, men, women, and children. Nothing else will reach the root of this case.[31]

The railroad and stagecoach companies sent lobbyists to Washington to urge the Congress to act to suppress the rampaging Indians. Clearly, something would have to be done. As an immediate result of the Fetterman Massacre, in 1867, George Armstrong Custer received his orders to take his first command on the Great Plains.[32]

THE POWDER RIVER WAR

To the whites, the Fetterman Massacre had been engineered by the wily Red Cloud, who they now saw as the preeminent Sioux leader. One contemporary observer noted, "Red Cloud, who had been one of the sub-chiefs of the Sioux, gained so much prestige by the defeat and slaughter of Fetterman's men that he became at once the leading war chief of the nation."[1]

Actually, Red Cloud, then about forty-five years old, had not taken an active role in the fighting. However, he took the credit. He was clearly the unifying force behind the Indian warriors in the Fetterman fight, but all the Indians knew that the genius behind their victory was their mystical war chief, Crazy Horse.

Indeed, Crazy Horse was a strange and complex man. Aside from a few friends like Hump and his brother Little Hawk, Crazy Horse was a loner. He walked around the village in stony silence, lost in his own thoughts. His second cousin Black Elk was a youngster when Crazy Horse became famous among the Oglalas. As an old man in the 1930s he recalled that he sometimes ate with his cousin in his lodge, and that Crazy Horse often teased him. As Black Elk said,

I was not afraid that he would hurt me; I was just afraid. Everybody felt that way about him, for he was a queer man and would go about the village without noticing people or saying anything. In his own teepee he would joke, and when he was on the warpath with a small party, he would joke to make his warriors feel good. But around the village he hardly ever noticed anybody, except little children. . . . He never joined a dance, and they say nobody ever heard him sing. But everybody liked him, and they would do anything he wanted or go any-where he said. He was a small man among the Lakotas and he was slender and had a thin face and his eyes looked through things and he always seemed to be thinking hard about something. He never wanted to have many things for himself, and did not have many ponies like a chief. They say that when game was scarce and the people were hungry, he would not eat at all. He was a queer man. Maybe he was always part way into that world of his vision.[2]

The winter of 1866–67 following the Fetterman fight was one of the fiercest winters on record, with endless snow-storms and little game. Black Elk recalled that the Oglalas broke camp soon after the battle and that, "The snow was very deep and it was very cold. . . . We were going away from where the soldiers were, and I do not know where we went but it was west. It was a hungry winter, for the deep snow made it hard to find elk . . . and also many of the people went snowblind."[3]

Because of the hard weather, Red Cloud and Crazy Horse had difficulty holding their vast fighting force together and the Indians soon scattered, divided into small bands held together either by their quest for a warmer campsite or the pursuit of game for their hungry families. Crazy Horse and Little Hawk did much of their hunting that winter on snowshoes, and once managed to kill eight elk with their hunting knives.[4]

In the spring of 1867 Crazy Horse and Little Hawk

rejoined Red Cloud to harass the soldiers in the Fort Phil Kearny region. The Sioux again made the Powder River country difficult for travelers. They planned another summer of raiding, joined by young warriors from Fort Laramie and some of Spotted Tail's discontented Brulés. But the Oglalas had no knowledge of what was going on in Washington, where politics had taken over the problem of the Plains Indians.

In June of 1867, President Andrew Johnson sent a new set of peace commissioners to Fort Laramie. Under pressure from eastern humanitarian groups such as the Quakers and many former abolitionist organizations, the Johnson administration was moving to take the situation out of the hands of the military and reach a peaceful resolution under the auspices of the Interior Department's Bureau of Indian Affairs. The Indian Bureau had seized the opportunity to discredit the army's treatment of the Indians and actually blamed the Fetterman Massacre on the soldiers. Thus, while General Sherman attempted to carry out one policy, the government, led by the Interior Department, embarked on another and attempted to block Sherman at every juncture.

The Interior Department's Commissioner of Indian Affairs, Lewis Bogy, was a Confederate sympathizer who disliked the army. Bogy had little affection for General Sherman, whom he recalled as the scourge of the South. Bogy's view was that if the army got control of the Indian problem, a disastrous and expensive war would be the result. In addition, Bogy worried that ultimately the Indians would be wiped out.

After the Civil War many Americans viewed military solutions to problems with distrust. This discomfort has lasted until our own time. Thus, while Sherman wanted direct action against the Sioux, the politicians, responding to a nervous electorate, saw to it that he lacked the military resources necessary to patrol and pacify the vast western territory.

The Interior Department mapped out a new solution

to the problem of warring Indian tribes on the Great Plains—the "reservation theory." Since a policy of "extermination"—not unpopular among some military men and in the west—was unconscionable (not to mention un-American), the department postulated that the best way "to save the Indians from extinction" was "to consolidate them as rapidly as can be peacefully done, on large reservations, from which all whites except Government employees would be excluded." In other words, for their own good the Plains Indians would be placed in protective custody by the government, thus removing them from the main roads of western settlement and, at the same time, saving the United States Treasury the expense of a protracted and bloody Indian war. As historian Edward Lazarus observed, "It was much cheaper to feed the Indians than to fight them, cheaper to kill a culture than a people."[5]

Thus, by mid-1867 the government embarked upon a policy of peace with the Indians, even though Red Cloud and Crazy Horse were still making life difficult for the settlers and soldiers on the frontier. A special commission appointed by Congress to investigate the Fetterman fiasco decided that the fault was with the government for establishing the Powder River Road and building new forts, and that peace with the Sioux would be impossible unless the road into Sioux country was abandoned. The commission even exonerated the Indians for wiping out Fetterman and his men by concluding, "They admit their inferiority to us in all respects and seem now to have gone to war for the purpose of averting the death and destruction of their race." By July 1867 both houses of Congress passed a bill authorizing the peace commissioners, who had already left, to travel west to seek peace with the warring Plains tribes.[6]

Over the summer of 1867 the peace commissioners traveled widely. On June 12 they met with Old-Man-Afraid-of-Horses, the Oglala chief at Fort Laramie. Red Cloud was present but stayed in the background, watching carefully that no treaties were negotiated without his approval. Eventually, after haggling over ammunition, which the whites did not want to give the Indians, Old-Man-Afraid walked out. In October they traveled to the north country to meet with Sitting Bull's wild Hunkpapas and then back again to Fort Laramie for meetings with Crazy Horse's uncle, Spotted Tail, who still led the Brulés.[7]

Spotted Tail, who wasn't considered a hostile, told the peace commission, "We object to the Powder River road. The country which we live in is cut up by the white men, who drive away all the game. That is the cause of our troubles."

The next day General Sherman, who accompanied the commission, answered for the whites. Chomping down hard on his ever present cigar, Sherman stared at the Sioux leaders, saying sternly,

> The United States cannot abandon its road across your country, but it will pay for any damage done by the Bozeman Trail. . . . You must learn to live like white men and we will help you for as long as you need—just as we helped the Cherokee, Creeks and Choctaws. We will set aside land for you, land for farming, housing and cattle-raising and we will teach your children to read and write. The railroads are coming, and you cannot stop [them] any more than you can stop the sun or the moon. You must decide; you must submit. This is not a peace commission only; it is also a war commission. Without peace, the Great Father who, out of love for you, withheld his soldiers, will let loose his young men and you will be swept away. . . .[8]

When the peace commission returned in November, not even the peaceful Sioux chiefs showed up to meet with them. Red Cloud, who had heard of Sherman's threats, refused to sign a treaty and sent a message from his safe camp near the Powder River: "If the Great Father kept white men out of my country, then peace would last forever. The Great Spirit has raised me in this land. . . . What I have said I mean. I mean to keep this land."[9]

Crazy Horse was adamantly opposed to any peace with the whites and spent much of the summer continuing his hit-and-run war. His warriors struck in eastern Wyoming and occasionally returned to Fort Kearney to try to lure the soldiers, now more cautious, into another trap.

Around the same time, in June of 1867, George Armstrong Custer, an ambitious young lieutenant colonel who had made a reputation during the Civil War, galloped across the prairie from Fort Hayes in Kansas to take command of three hundred cavalrymen marching toward Fort McPherson in Nebraska to search out hostile Indians. When Custer reached Fort McPherson he proceeded to insult the commanding officer, Colonel Henry Carrington, by refusing his invitation for dinner. Custer felt contempt for the old officer who had been so humiliated by Crazy Horse and Red Cloud that he had been relieved of his command at Fort Phil Kearny and shifted to the more placid Platte River area. The fact that Carrington, who had the experience of combat with Crazy Horse and Red Cloud, could inform Custer of their tactics was meaningless to the headstrong young officer. Custer wasn't interested in hearing anything from a man for whom he had no respect.[10]

Back in the Powder River country many younger Sioux warriors were turning to Crazy Horse for leadership. Some had grown suspicious of Red Cloud because of his interest in peace talks. The Oglala Sioux, still under the direction of Red Cloud, were launching new, prolonged attacks against the soldier forts in the north country. On the Powder River, Red Cloud's powerful forces split up. At the Bighorn, several hundred warriors, mostly Cheyenne, attacked a soldier party outside Fort C. F. Smith, and on August 2, 1867, over a thousand Oglala braves in war paint and splendid battle regalia attacked a party of woodcutters near Fort Phil Kearny.

This time the woodcutters were guarded by a detachment of soldiers armed with new 50-caliber breech-loading Springfield rifles, and the Wagon Box Fight, as it came to be called, did not go well for the Sioux. The soldiers placed

Armed with new 50-caliber breech-loading Springfield rifles, U.S. soldiers held off Crazy Horse and his warriors in the Wagon Box Fight, August 2, 1867.

fourteen wagon boxes in a circle after removing their wheels. As the Indians attacked, the soldiers crawled into the protective boxes, out of arrow range. Crazy Horse and Hump led the attack but their warriors were unable to close in as the soldiers, protected by the thickness of the boxes, opened up a continuous line of rifle fire. Even though the sight of a thousand Indians riding down on the circle of wagon boxes must have been terrifying, the soldiers stayed under cover as their shelters began to look like huge pincushions with many arrows sticking out of them.[11]

With little real firepower, the Oglala's desperate horseback charges were futile. An exasperated Crazy Horse declared, "We are butchered like the spotted buffalo without ammunition!"[12]

Crazy Horse ordered his warriors to withdraw when he learned that a hundred soldiers were on their way from Fort Phil Kearny to relieve the besieged men in the wagon boxes. The Indians lost six dead and six were wounded, with the whites suffering slightly higher casualties. But the commander of the Wagon Box fight, Captain J. N. Powell, reported to General Sherman that the soldiers had killed sixty Sioux. The story spread and inflated across the frontier, with reports that hundreds of Indians had been killed. Eventually, some writers claimed that Red Cloud had lost 1,500 warriors in the fight. The Sioux laughed when they heard the distorted numbers from passing traders that winter, and Crazy Horse himself wondered, "How can they say these foolish things? Do they not know that we are the same ones as last winter, when the hundred soldiers were left on the ground?"[13]

General Sherman knew better. While the battle was a loss for the Sioux, Sherman knew that Red Cloud had the numbers to make him impossible to check unless he was defeated in battle. And Sherman also knew that Congress would not give him the funds to raise a force that could defeat Red Cloud and his Oglalas. Ever the military realist, Sherman now moved into the camp of those who sought a peace treaty with the warring Sioux.

Crazy Horse spent the winter of 1867–68 doing what he loved best: hunting and providing sustenance for the helpless and needy among his people. When spring broke it was apparent that the Powder River War had settled into a stalemate. Few whites dared to travel the Bozeman Trail, and the Sioux were equally unwilling to lose any more warriors in futile attacks against the well-supplied and fortified soldier outposts.[14]

In the spring of 1868, General Sherman resumed attempts at making peace with the Sioux. Sherman was convinced that once the railroad had completed its westward push, the buffalo hunters would follow and they would finish the work of the military. To Sherman and other military leaders, the destruction of the great buffalo herds was the surest way to end the Indian wars and to break the Plains Indians. As General Phil Sheridan testified to the Texas state legislature when they were debating a bill to protect the endangered buffalo,

> *Instead of stopping the hunters you ought to give them a hearty vote of thanks, and give each hunter a medal of bronze with a dead buffalo on one side and a discouraged Indian on the other. These men have done more in the last two years, and will do more in the next year, to settle the vexed Indian question than the regular army has done in the last thirty. They are destroying the Indian commissary....*[15]

Finally, on April 29, 1868, the peace commissioners again returned to Fort Laramie for another meeting with the chieftains of the Brulé, Oglala, Minniconjou, and Yanktoni branches of the Sioux nation. The tribal leaders accepted a treaty that provided for a vast reservation of all the land making up the present state of South Dakota west of the Missouri River.

The tribes also insisted that they be allowed to hunt buffalo in the territory north of the North Platte and on the Republican River. The treaty guaranteed the Indians that right as long as the buffalo lasted in that region. Thus, all the land between their sacred Black Hills to the Bighorn Mountain range (the Powder River country) became "unceded Indian territory" with the proviso that no whites would be permitted entry without consent by the Sioux.

Neither General Sherman nor Red Cloud appeared for the signing and thus there was still a measure of discomfort on both sides. Sherman did not like the buffalo clause, and Red Cloud would never sign a treaty that allowed the hated forts to remain along the Bozeman Trail.[16]

Finally, to the dismay of many in the military, General Sherman relented and agreed to abandon the forts. On July 29, 1868, the troops at Fort C. F. Smith marched away. The next morning Crazy Horse and his warriors burned the fort

In 1868 at Fort Laramie, Wyoming Territory, the Sioux and the U.S. government signed a treaty reserving most of the present state of South Dakota as Sioux territory forever. In this photograph representatives meet in a tent to sign the treaty (General William T. Sherman, seated in the tent, can be identified by his white beard).

to the ground. A few days later the soldiers abandoned Forts Reno and Phil Kearny. The triumphant Sioux burned those forts too. On November 4, Red Cloud was proudly accompanied to Fort Laramie by 125 tribal leaders representing Oglala, Hunkpapa, Sans Arc, and other great tribes of the Plains. On November 6, 1868, Red Cloud "touched the pen" to the treaty paper. The Powder River War was over as Red Cloud became the first and only Indian in the West to defeat the government of the United States in a war.[17]

Not every Sioux was happy with the new peace. Red

Cloud told the whites that it would be difficult for him to control his younger warriors, but he promised that he would never again make war on the whites. And, after a trip in 1870 to the White House and a meeting with President Ulysses S. Grant where Red Cloud came to grasp the full power of the whites, he never did.[18]

The 1868 treaty was made to be broken. The whites thought that the Indians would keep their promise by agreeing to those portions of the treaty the government called "civilizing." Some of these included giving up warring against other tribes, relinquishing the Sun Dance and other sacred rituals, accepting instruction in Christianity from missionaries, and schooling for their children. However, the Sioux later claimed they did not understand that they had agreed to become farmers when the buffalo disappeared. In addition, there were complicated provisions requiring the government to provide them with wagons, animals, plows, and other agricultural implements that would somehow turn a spirited nomadic people into productive farmers. The treaty insisted upon compulsory education for the Indian children as if the act of giving them haircuts, putting them in little red schoolhouses, and teaching them to read the whites' Bible and other books, would cure them of being Indians.

Demonstrating their ignorance of Indian life and tribal structure, the United States government insisted that if the Sioux sought to revise the treaty, no changes could be made without the approval of three-fourths of the adult male Sioux population. How the bureaucrats who drew up this treaty could have imagined getting a scattered population to agree to anything in large numbers challenges the imagination.

Most disturbing of all, the whites still did not understand that no single Sioux leader spoke for all the Sioux. Certainly, the politically savvy Red Cloud was not signing a treaty in behalf of war leaders like Crazy Horse and Sitting Bull, the leading Hunkpapa, who rejected the treaty. As Crazy Horse said,

Now you tell us to work for a living, but the Great Spirit did not make us to work but to live by hunting. You white men can work if you want to. We do not interfere with you, and again you say, why do you not become civilized? We do not want your civilization. We would live as our fathers lived, and their fathers before them.[19]

The younger Sioux warriors now turned for leadership to Crazy Horse for the Oglalas and Sitting Bull for the Hunkpapas. But by 1869, the battle for the land was essentially over. By signing the treaty Red Cloud had effectively split the Lakota (Sioux) nation in two. There were few places in the west where Indians were truly free as they had been in the past. As the historian Dee Brown observed, "The audacity of the American character came out in this period. It wasn't all evil. But it was partly evil."[20]

For his part, Crazy Horse had mixed feelings for he had limited knowledge of the whites and of their capabilities. In his view, he had led his people successfully against the Crows and had driven them from what was now Oglala land. He had been a pivotal war leader under Red Cloud, and prevented the whites from penetrating the Powder River country. From this perspective, he had been successful. He was not free to roam and hunt where he chose, except in the region south of the Platte River. But what did that matter? The Sioux lands were vast, game was still plentiful, and Crazy Horse was free along with his family, friends, and followers to be whatever he wished. It was all, however, a heartbreaking illusion. Crazy Horse may have been a valiant warrior and brilliant tactician on the field of battle; but he may still have been naive when it came to understanding whites or estimating the military force they could bring against his people.

CHAPTER EIGHT

TO THE LITTLE BIGHORN

The only good Indians I ever saw were dead.
—*General Philip H. Sheridan, 1869*

One does not sell the land the people walk on.
—*Crazy Horse, 1875*

Crazy Horse and his followers spent much of 1869 in the Powder River region, far removed from any contact with whites. They hunted and on occasion, as in the old days, went out on small raiding parties against their traditional enemies, the Crows and Shoshonis.

By the fall, the Oglalas had accumulated many buffalo hides and valuable furs as news came that the white traders, encouraged by the truce resulting from the treaty, were again traveling up the Platte River. The Indians were pleased to once again trade with the whites. There had been no trading since 1864 and the Sioux were eager for the wide variety of goods they offered.[1]

However, General Sherman's attitude was tough when it came to dealing with the Indians. Sherman believed that if the Indians wanted the whites' goods, they would have to show good faith by moving to the established government reservations. If the Indians insisted on their freedom, however, they would have it without any commerce or help from the whites. Thus, when a band of Oglalas traveled to the Platte River region to trade, the soldiers, under orders from Sherman, fired on them, wounding one and forcing the others to retreat. Sherman was adamant. There would be no trading with nontreaty Indians along the North Platte River.[2]

When told that the whites had fired on the Oglalas, Crazy Horse was not surprised. He had little faith or trust in whites and remarked, "Ahh-h, it is a bad way to do!"[3] He knew the troubles were far from over, even with Red Cloud's peace. He had heard the terrible news that the new white commander, Custer, called, "Long Hair" by the Sioux, had slaughtered Black Kettle's peaceful band of southern Cheyenne on the Washita River near the Oklahoma–Kansas border. Survivors of the Washita Massacre had joined the Oglalas in the Powder River country. They told Crazy Horse and the other chiefs that only a few weeks after Red Cloud had signed the treaty, in late November 1868, Custer and his troops swept down on the village, slaughtering women and children as well as over a hundred Cheyenne warriors.

So much has been written about George Armstrong Custer that it is difficult to separate fact from myth. Ralph K. Andrist writes, "Custer was a man of supreme physical courage who apparently did not know what it was to feel fear." Custer had graduated at the very bottom of his class (thirty-fourth out of thirty-four cadets) at West Point. He received his commission just in time to get into the First Battle of Bull Run during the Civil War, where he impressed his superiors with his boldness and bravery. However, Custer had a reputation for impulsiveness that outweighed any skills he had as a military tactician. He was at his best, it was said, when "leading a cavalry charge, saber swinging, yellow hair streaming in the wind, the field behind him thundering with hundreds of men and horses answering to his command. . . ."[4]

Another scholar, Paul Andrew Hutton, wrote,

Cocky, reckless, and headstrong, Custer poses for a photograph before going west to assume a command in the army's campaign against the Indians.

George Armstrong Custer loved war. It was a tonic to him. Whereas others shrank from its ghastly carnage, he reveled in it. It often seemed, in fact, that only when dealing with death could he truly come alive. War not only brought him national acclaim and high rank but also gave him a power that peace denied him. For only through displays of the most reckless courage was he able to impress, even inspire, others.[5]

Custer's worst problems on the plains were with his troops. He was a harsh taskmaster: many of his men did not like him, and many deserted. He had survived a court-martial in 1867, with a one-year suspension from duty, for shooting deserters (which somewhat solved Custer's desertion problems), and he had been denounced in the northern press for flogging soldiers who stepped out of line.

Custer's views about Indians (and about blacks, too), reflected racist ideas and the typical unenlightened attitudes of many mid-nineteenth-century Americans: that the Indians were an inferior, backward, and uncivilized race. He wrote of them as "bloodthirsty barbarians" or "savages." Yet in "The Red Man," an 1868 essay, Custer called the Sioux and other Indians noble savages "on the verge of extinction." Also, he admired their great stamina for long marches, and respected their courage and ability as fighters.[6]

Thus, while he was their major antagonist in the last great conflict between the Indian and the whites for the West, Custer sympathized with their struggle. In his 1874 autobiography, *My Life on the Plains*, Custer wrote with empathy of the war leader Crazy Horse, and his powerful desire to live a free and untrammeled life on the Great Plains.

If I were an Indian, I often think that I would greatly prefer to cast my lot among those of my people who adhered to the free open plains, rather than submit to the confined limits of a reservation there to be the recip-

ient of the blessed benefits of civilization, with its vices thrown in without stint or measure.[7]

On November 27, 1868, Custer and the Seventh Cavalry hit a southern Cheyenne village camped along the Washita River in what is today northern Oklahoma. Despite the treaty, the Cheyenne, southern Oglalas, Arapaho, and other Plains tribes were still on the warpath, and younger warriors often conducted raids into Kansas and Texas. Once again the army made no distinction between the young renegades and the Indians who kept the peace. General Philip H. Sheridan ordered Custer and his Seventh Cavalry to attack any villages thought to be harboring renegades in the vicinity of Fort Cobb, which had been set up to provide food and protection to friendly Indians. As one scholar noted, "Any warriors not killed in battle were to be hanged; all women and children were to be taken prisoner; all villages destroyed, and all ponies killed. These were brutally explicit orders. Sherman could lose his temper and talk about extermination; Sheridan could coldly put extermination into effect."[8]

With Civil War general Ulysses S. Grant as the new president-elect, delighted military leaders on the frontier hardly concealed how they felt and how they planned to deal with the remaining hostiles. When General Sheridan met the Comanche chief Toch-a-way ("Turtle Dove") at Fort Cobb shortly after the Washita Massacre, the Indian introduced himself saying, "Me Toch-a-way, me good Indian." Sheridan coldly replied, "The only good Indians I ever saw were dead."[9]

Comfortable with his orders to search out and destroy hostiles, Custer led the assault on the Cheyenne camped by the Washita River. At the break of dawn, in the icy cold, to the tune "Garry Owen" (which his buglers could barely blow as their saliva froze in their bugles), the Seventh Cavalry swept down on Black Kettle's sleeping Cheyenne village. Custer most likely had no idea where he was, or how many Indians were there, or even who these Indians were. He was simply intent on making his name and impressing his two commanders, General Sherman and General Sheridan. Custer split his forces and the soldiers shot everything that moved.[10]

Custer's official report listed 103 warriors killed. There was, however, no mention of the thirty-eight women and children also gunned down, or that Custer had strangely abandoned a detachment of nineteen troopers under the command of Major Joel Elliott, who chased after the escaping Cheyenne. They were later found killed and mutilated. No one has ever accused Custer of cowardice in leaving Elliott and his men surrounded by enraged Indians, yet their abandonment was never explained. As one historian wrote, the episode "might be called Custer's first stand."[11]

This time the unfortunate Black Kettle, a survivor of Sand Creek, was killed, and for good measure Custer slaughtered a herd of over 600 ponies, turning the surviving Cheyenne into paupers. The following day Custer boasted of his triumph in a letter to General Sheridan: "We have cleaned Black Kettle and his band out so thoroughly that they can neither fight, dress, sleep, eat [n]or ride without sponging upon their friends."[12]

In the east, humanitarian groups compared the Washita massacre to Sand Creek. But General Sheridan was delighted and issued a general field order in praise of Custer. Noting that captives and stolen horses proved that the village was a war camp, he said,

> I am well satisfied with Custer's attack, and would not have wept if he had served Satanta and Bull Bear's band in the same style. I want you to go ahead; kill and punish the hostile, rescue the captive white women and children, capture and destroy the ponies. . . .[13]

However, the fate of Major Elliott and his men bothered many soldiers in the field, and some viewed Custer, whose star may have risen with the general staff, with skepticism and disdain. Washita had propelled the "Boy General" to fame and national notoriety which was, after all, what Custer wanted. He returned to his wife, Libbie, at Fort Hayes for the summer of 1869. For the next two years, Custer would bask in the attention given him as "a famous Indian fighter."[14]

Meanwhile, the change of administrations in Washington, D.C., marked a subtle shift in government policy toward the Indians. Crazy Horse and his Oglalas could not know that the forces of history and politics were now converging to change the Sioux way of life forever. The Grant administration, perhaps the most corrupt in American history, would make no exception in its heavy and underhanded dealings with the Indians of the western plains.

With Ulysses S. Grant in the White House, changes came quickly. Approximately 250,000 Indians in the United States still fell within the scope of federal policy. The vast majority were west of the Mississippi. By Grant's election in 1868, the Bureau of Indian Affairs, under the jurisdiction of the Department of the Interior since 1849, had become the employer of political hacks and the party faithful who had helped elect the president. With little coordination between the Bureau of Indian Affairs in Washington and its field agencies on the frontier, the Bureau became, in the words of one scholar, "a morass of corruption and inefficiency."[15]

On December 6, 1869, in an address to Congress, President Grant explained his Indian policy. After reviewing the terrible history of the government's relationship with the tribes, Grant said that he had "attempted a new policy towards these wards of the nation (they cannot be regarded in any other light than as wards) with fair results so far tried. . . ." His new "Peace Policy" would be to place the Indians on reservations as quickly as possible and to introduce a system where they could ultimately be the beneficiaries of a land policy with some form of territorial government.[16]

Grant's policy did not work. From 1869 to 1871 there was little improvement in the government's relations with the Indians. To restrict thousands of Native Americans, who had been living freely for centuries, to reservations to become peaceful farmers was an absurd idea. To think that they might easily surrender and give their lives over to corrupt and fraudulent agents who became rich while they starved was ridiculous.

In the Southwest, by the early summer of 1870, the first fruits of the Grant administration's new Indian policy became painfully apparent as the Kiowas, Comanches, and Cheyenne furiously fought the government. In the Arizona territory, the Apache tribes led by Cochise and Geronimo made relentless war on whites. The situation became so intolerable by 1870 that some high officials talked about setting up an Indian state within the boundaries of the United States.[17]

For Crazy Horse and his Oglala followers in the Powder River country, the years between 1869 and 1871 were relatively free from contact with whites and from military intrusion. The soldiers were busy quelling disturbances on the southwestern frontier and left the northern Sioux to live as "peacefully" as they had always lived, while making war on their traditional enemies.

During this time a number of tragic events occurred that were to shape the remainder of Crazy Horse's life. In the late fall of 1870, Crazy Horse and Hump led a war party against the Shoshone. But the Oglalas found themselves outnumbered and outgunned by a superior force. Years later, He Dog, an Oglala warrior who participated in the raid, described the event. As He Dog remembered it, Crazy Horse and Hump had disagreed. Hump argued to stay and fight, to preserve their honor and good names. But Crazy Horse, the master tactical fighter, said, "We will fight, but I think we will get a whipping. . . . It's a bad place for a fight and a bad day for it, and the enemy are twelve to our one."

In the battle, with the Oglalas using bows and arrows against the Shoshone rifles, the Sioux were overwhelmed. Hump shouted to Crazy Horse, "We are up against it now! My horse is wounded in the leg." "I know it," Crazy Horse shouted back. "We were up against it from the start." Then

Hump was surrounded by a sea of Shoshone warriors. Crazy Horse charged in shouting and shooting his revolver, but was too late to save his friend, who fell from his wounded horse and lay dead on the ground.[18]

Crazy Horse tried to fight on but an Oglala warrior called Good Weasel grabbed the reins of his pony and yelled that the loss of one good Oglala brave was enough, and he led Crazy Horse away from the battle. After a few days, Crazy Horse went back to find Hump's body, accompanied by his brother-in-law, Red Feather. Years later, Red Feather recalled,

> Four days later Crazy Horse and I went back to find Hump and bury him. We didn't find anything but the skull and a few bones. Hump had been eaten by coyotes already. There weren't any Shoshonis around. When the Shoshonis found out whom they had killed, they beat it.[19]

Hump had been like a father to Crazy Horse since he was a small boy. He had been his teacher, mentor, and most trusted friend. Crazy Horse returned to his village stricken with grief. He was, now more than ever, a man alone, and the loss of Hump may have been a factor in the following event.

Shortly after Hump's death (the exact date is not known), Crazy Horse decided to make Black Buffalo Woman his wife. Apparently, Crazy Horse and Black Buffalo Woman had been carrying on an adulterous affair for many years. As He Dog said years later, "Crazy Horse had been paying open attention to the woman for a long time." Adultery, while not uncommon among the Sioux, was frowned upon. Still, a woman was permitted to change her mind about husbands and divorce was always a possibility.[20]

Although she had three children, Black Buffalo Woman left her husband, No Water, and moved in with Crazy Horse. No Water took the news of his wife's action badly and came after them. One night when Crazy Horse was camped along the Powder River, No Water caught up to him as he and Black Buffalo Woman were eating dinner in a friend's lodge. No Water rushed in crying, "My friend, I have come!" Crazy Horse went for his knife but his friend, Little Big Man, caught his arm. Black Buffalo Woman screamed as No Water fired a revolver he had borrowed from Bad Heart Bull. The bullet hit Crazy Horse below the left nostril and fractured his jaw as he fell forward into the campfire. If it hadn't been for the intimidating presence of Crazy Horse's giant friend, Touch-the-Clouds, a second bullet would have finished him off. Black Buffalo Woman, afraid for her life, fled and returned to live with her relatives. No Water, convinced he had killed the great "akicita" of the Sioux and an Oglala leader as well, jumped on the nearest pony and rode off.[21]

In the village the women began to wail and shriek: "Crazy Horse dead! Our Strange Man killed in an Oglala camp!" Crazy Horse was not dead but he was seriously wounded. However, the most serious wound may have been political. No Water was closely connected to Red Cloud and the incident could have split the Oglala Sioux when tribal unity was crucial against the white threat. Friends of Crazy Horse went out to kill No Water. When they couldn't find him they killed his mule. A serious intertribal feud had begun.

Eventually, No Water, who had violated tribal law by his attack on Crazy Horse, apologized and sent Crazy Horse a gift of ponies. Although Crazy Horse accepted the gift, he had not gotten over the loss of Black Buffalo Woman and one day attacked No Water. As a result, he was removed as an Oglala Shirt-Wearer. Soon the entire structure of tribal governance broke down. The Big Bellies, who appointed the Shirt-Wearers, could not agree on who would replace Crazy Horse and they stopped meeting. As Stephen E. Ambrose says, "The Oglalas had made a promising start in the development of a governmental organization that would have made it possible for them to act together in the face of an outside threat. Now that hope was gone." Black Buffalo Woman returned to her husband

and later had a fourth child, a girl with very light hair. Oglala rumor had it that the child's father was Crazy Horse.[22] From this point on, there was bad blood between the followers of Red Cloud and those who supported Crazy Horse. Later, this rift would have serious implications.

Crazy Horse slowly recovered. Although he could not speak, he used sign language to tell his friends that there should be no trouble and that Black Buffalo Woman should not be punished. Sometime in 1871, when his wound had healed, he joined a buffalo hunt along the Yellowstone River. Crazy Horse had barely settled in when he was hit with yet another great tragedy.

On the way home with a war party that had gone up against the Shoshone in the south, the Oglalas were ambushed by white miners. In the ensuing battle Little Hawk, the brother of Crazy Horse, was killed. Again, as after Hump's death, Crazy Horse fell into a depression. The little brother who had been his pupil and trusted comrade in battle and adventure on the plains was gone forever. As Mari Sandoz wrote, "as Crazy Horse realized what had been done a dust-grey bitterness settled in his heart, a bitterness that would take a long time to be gone."[23]

Shortly afterward, in the summer of 1872, Crazy Horse married Black Shawl, the sister of his friend, Red Feather. Perhaps the loss of Black Buffalo Woman and the deaths of Hump and Little Hawk made Crazy Horse seek some attachment. His mother helped to arrange the marriage, at Crazy Horse's request. "You must say there will be little joy in life with me," he told his mother. Soon Crazy Horse and Black Shawl had a daughter they called They-Are-Afraid-of-Her. Crazy Horse doted on the child, playing with her for hours and telling her stories. He became known as a storyteller among the village children. Black Elk was among the children who listened to his stories and he later recalled how Crazy Horse was drawn to children.[24]

Once again tragedy struck. Crazy Horse's little girl died of cholera in the summer of 1874. Crazy Horse was away on a raid against the Crows. When he returned, his father told him of the child's death. Crazy Horse's grief was boundless. Although his daughter's burial scaffold was deep in Crow country, some seventy miles from where Crazy Horse was camped near the Little Bighorn River, Crazy Horse was determined to see his beloved daughter one last time. Accompanied by an old friend, a white scout named Frank Grouard, Crazy Horse set out for Crow country. He found his daughter's death scaffold and, according to Grouard, he climbed up with the dead child, lay down beside her, and mourned for three days and nights.

According to Oglalas who knew Crazy Horse, he was not the same after the death of They-Are-Afraid-of-Her. During the next year and a half, through the winter of 1875–76, Crazy Horse would be seen riding out of the Oglala camp alone. He disappeared for weeks at a time and no one knew where he went or what he did. There are records that during this period dozens of white miners who were violating the Treaty of 1868 and crossing over into the Black Hills were found dead with an arrow stuck into the ground beside their bodies. And, curiously, none of the dead men had been scalped.[25]

Despite his personal tragedies, Crazy Horse could hardly escape the fact that, although he was no longer a Shirt-Wearer, many Oglalas and other Sioux unhappy with the Treaty of 1868 still looked to him for leadership. In the early 1870s two events tested that leadership. The first was the destruction of the buffalo herds. The treaty of 1868 allowed the Sioux to live outside the government reservations as long as there were a sufficient number of buffalo to sustain their nomadic needs. Although great herds numbering in the millions still roamed the northern central plains through the 1870s, the herds were thinning, and the buffalo were becoming harder to find. White buffalo hunters like William F. "Buffalo Bill" Cody streamed into the region on the Union Pacific Railroad and slaughtered the herds for their hides. These hunters killed up to three million buffalo a year in the early 1870s, threatening the lifestyle, the economy, and the survival of the Plains Indi-

A harvest of buffalo skulls: by the latter half of the nineteenth century, white settlers and bounty hunters had killed the buffalo to the edge of extinction.

ans. General Philip Sheridan, exhibiting an attitude typical of the military, said, "If I could learn that every buffalo in the northern herd were killed I would be glad. The destruction of this herd would do more to keep Indians quiet than anything else that could happen."[26]

The second important event in the 1870s was the discovery of gold in the Black Hills of South Dakota. Under the treaty this was the very heart of Sioux territory, and the Sioux Nation held the Black Hills, the "Paha Sapa," as sacred land.[27] White prospectors told wild tales of the riches in the Dakota territory, and pressure built on the Grant administration to open up the area. The Panic of 1873, an economic depression, and efforts of railroaders, farmers, immigrant groups, and the ever present army, pushed the administration to ignore the Sioux Treaty of 1868.[28]

Thus, in 1874, in blatant violation of the 1868 treaty and with the enthusiastic support of his military superiors and their political bosses all the way to the White House, General Phil Sheridan sent troops into the Black Hills to build a fort to protect the gold miners and prospectors. The unstated purpose of this expedition was to take as much gold as possible out of the sacred Sioux lands.

To provide an excuse for breaking the treaty, Sheridan noted that the Sioux had been attacking settlers in northern Nebraska and harassing the railroads. But this was either an exaggeration or a lie, because in 1873 Sheridan himself stated in an official report that "The condition of Indian affairs in the Department of Dakota has been remarkably quiet. . . ." So, on July 2, 1874, a column of over one thousand men and two thousand horses and mules marched out of Fort Abraham Lincoln on the Missouri River, just south of Bismarck, North Dakota. To the jolly lilt of "Garry Owen," they headed for the Black Hills. Accompanying the soldiers were sixty to a hundred Indian scouts, a team of expert miners, newspaper reporters, a photographer, and orders to gather military and scientific information about the region. Perched high on his bay, wearing fringed buckskins, his long light-colored hair flowing out from under a felt hat, rode the commander of the column, the dashing Lieutenant Colonel George Armstrong Custer.[29]

Custer was not new to battling Indians. In 1873 he had met Crazy Horse and his warriors in a tough fight in the Yellowstone Valley, where Custer had been sent to protect surveyor teams mapping the way west for the railroad. However, these battles were inconclusive and eventually Custer withdrew from the area; the Sioux, led by Sitting Bull and Crazy Horse, returned to the Powder River country. Custer was convinced that he had driven the Indians away from the northern construction of the railroad; the Indians believed they had repulsed the soldiers because for two years there were no further expeditions into the Yellowstone area. Now, the ambitious Custer saw himself headed for fame and glory—a frontier trailblazer going to the Black Hills, which were, he wrote, "as yet unseen by human eyes except those of the Indians."[30]

As Alvin M. Josephy has written, "Custer's invasion was as deliberate an incitement to trouble with Indians as was ever committed." The Sioux carefully observed the Custer expedition and used smoke signals to warn that a vast contingent of bluecoats was entering sacred Sioux lands. Custer's force was too strong and well armed for the Sioux to attack. However, the main fighting strength of the hostile Sioux, led by Sitting Bull and Crazy Horse, may not have received the warning for they were camped far to the west in the Bighorn mountains. By the time Crazy Horse found out that Custer had invaded the Black Hills, Custer was back inside Fort Abraham Lincoln.[31]

The Custer expedition was a great success. With little opposition, the soldiers spent their time picnicking, hunting (Custer himself killed a grizzly), and playing what was probably the first game of baseball in Sioux country. In addition, on July 27 the expedition found gold. When news of the find hit the telegraph wires, it was a nationwide invitation to anyone who desired to get rich quick. By the time Custer and his men returned to Fort Lincoln in late August, the gold rush was on.[32]

As prospectors streamed into the Black Hills in the fall of 1874, the American military made halfhearted efforts to keep them out. Crazy Horse led a war party to the region to harass the prospectors, but there were so many, he could accomplish little. When the cold weather set in, Crazy Horse returned to his camp for the winter to decide what to do about the latest white invasion.[33]

In the meantime, the wheels of the American military and the government began to grind, to find a basis for breaking the Treaty of 1868 and to relieve the Sioux, once and for all time, of their ancestral lands. Custer's reports helped to provide the Grant administration with some excuse for that action. The Indians were not using the Black Hills—therefore, it was not unreasonable to expect them to relinquish the lands. On September 8, 1874, Custer wrote to the War Department, "It is a mistaken idea that the Indian occupies any portion of the Black Hills. They neither occupy nor make use of the Black Hills, nor are they willing that others should. . . ."[34]

In the spring of 1875 the government made the first move. The Grant administration decided to acquire the Black Hills and invited Red Cloud and Spotted Tail, the two chiefs who had signed the treaty and had not violated the peace, back to Washington. The administration's strategy was to see if these chiefs were willing to sell out their people by selling the Black Hills as well as the Sioux claims to hunting rights along the Platte and Republican rivers. The Indians arrived in the nation's capital furious that the whites had violated the treaty, infesting their lands, they said, "like maggots." However, President Grant himself put it clearly to the Indian leaders. He warned them there would "be trouble in keeping white people from going [into the Black Hills] for gold." He threatened that "it is possible that strong efforts might not be made to keep them out" if the Sioux ultimately refused to sell their land.[35] When the chiefs returned from Washington they found the Sioux territory in chaos, with whites streaming into the Black Hills.

By 1875, after another severe winter, even the peaceful agency Sioux were disgruntled with their treatment by the whites. Many younger warriors began to leave the agency and rode north to join Crazy Horse. The goods the government sent the Sioux that winter of were of poor quality. The sacks of flour were small and moldy. The pork was rotten. The agent was obviously stealing, and to make their point, some of the Sioux butchered their own ponies for meat right in front of the fort.[36]

The government, to solve the problem, appointed another commission to negotiate with the Indians and on September 4, 1875, the commissioners reached the Red Cloud Agency where negotiations began two weeks later.[37] The problem was, who spoke for the Sioux Nation? The answer, the commissioners soon found out, was no one, and everyone, as some twenty thousand Sioux gathered to hear the American offer for the Black Hills country.

The commissioners found three distinct factions of Sioux. The first was Red Cloud's Oglalas and Spotted Tail's Brulés, who lived on government handouts and would not fight despite treaty violations. The second was the Sioux led by Young-Man-Afraid-of-Horses, who had followed his father to the Red Cloud Agency (where Red Cloud had gone to live and which bore his name because of his prominence as a Sioux leader). Young-Man-Afraid-of-Horses pledged not to fight anymore but steadfastly opposed the sale of the Black Hills. The third faction, led by Crazy Horse and Sitting Bull, was made up of Oglalas and Hunkpapas who were not simply opposed to selling the Black Hills—if they had to, they would fight to keep them.[38]

The commissioners met with many branches of the three factions within the Sioux Nation. Although Crazy Horse was not there, some of his warriors joined the thousands of others to listen to the government's offer. Among this group was Crazy Horse's friend Little Big Man, who came to the meeting wearing only an eagle feather warbonnet and a breechcloth. Perched bareback on his horse with a Winchester rifle in one hand and a fistful of bullets in the other, he rode directly into the meeting leading three hundred hostile Sioux painted for battle and chanting:

> Black Hills is my land and I love it
> And whoever interferes
> Will hear this gun.

No one knows whether Little Big Man was acting on the instructions of Crazy Horse, but Crazy Horse had made his feelings clear. When told of the projected sale of the Black Hills he had said, "One does not sell the land the people walk on." Little Big Man roared that he had come to kill the whites who were stealing the Indians' lands. "I will kill the first chief who speaks for selling the Black Hills!" he shouted.[39]

There were tense moments as Little Big Man's warriors circled the commissioners. Spotted Tail urged the commissioners to withdraw, afraid that the enraged Sioux would slaughter them on the spot. The situation was defused by Young-Man-Afraid-of-Horses who was still a friend of Crazy Horse. Young-Man-Afraid, the son of a respected chief, opposed the sale of the Black Hills. He ordered Little Big Man's warriors to cool off and, because he also headed a large force of Indian police, he was able to keep peace. Young-Man-Afraid knew that if the commissioners were hurt or killed, the whites would retaliate; in the end, all Sioux would suffer dreadfully.[40]

Ultimately, little was accomplished by the meeting. Red Cloud asked $600 million for the Black Hills. The commissioners countered with an offer of $6 million. The chiefs refused and the meeting ended. Was Red Cloud betraying his people by even offering to negotiate the sale of their precious Black Hills? Perhaps, in the eyes of Crazy Horse and Sitting Bull. But as Edward Lazarus noted, "Most of the Sioux . . . could not afford the luxury of outright refusal, however much they wished it possible. No longer self-supporting, they were trapped between ways of life, an old one loved, but to which they could never return, and a new one which seemed strange and unnatural but was perhaps the only way to survive."[41]

Another treaty was broken when white prospectors rushed into the Black Hills, South Dakota, to mine for gold. Army caravans were sent to protect the white prospectors from angered Indians.

The Grant administration was not to be deterred from finding a legal excuse to take the Black Hills from the Sioux. On November 3, 1875, at a Cabinet meeting with General Sheridan present, the president and his advisers decided that the key to taking over the Black Hills was the elimination of the hostiles. If they did not come voluntarily onto the reservation, they would be considered in violation of American law and subject to military action: the hostile Sioux would be driven out of the unceded territory in Wyoming and Montana. They would be forced, once and for all, to become reservation Indians by January 31, 1876; and, if they still refused, the United States Army would come after them, subdue them, and bring them in. Neither President Grant nor any of his closest advisers thought there would be much of a problem. After all, they reasoned, with tough military planners like Sherman and Sheridan, and field commanders like Custer, it would be easy to force the hostile Sioux onto government reservations. As historian Alvin M. Josephy, Jr., wrote, "Apparently few persons expected that the northern hostiles would risk a war with the formidable forces that would be thrown against them."[42]

The government even created its own strange rationale for going after the free Sioux in the unceded lands. After seven years of frustration—with Sioux hunting bands raiding the borders of the unceded territory; continuous attacks on friendly tribes such as the Crows; assaults on the Northern Pacific Railroad; recruitment of hostile agency Sioux, stealing supplies and munitions from the agencies; and interference with the sale of the Black Hills—the United States government would now hold the Indians accountable.[43]

The government would acquire the Black Hills and, at the same time, end the Indian way of life on the plains. For the Grant administration it was a solution to a vexing problem. But for the last real warriors of the once mighty Sioux Nation, it was a matter of life and death. That winter Crazy Horse moved his followers, numbering about a hundred lodges with between two and three hundred warriors, north to the Powder River region to talk to Sitting Bull and his Hunkpapas about guns and ammunition. Crazy Horse and Sitting Bull were going to fight.[44]

CHAPTER NINE

CRAZY HORSE
AND THE BATTLE OF
THE LITTLE BIGHORN

I could whip all the Indians on the Continent with the Seventh Cavalry.
—George Armstrong Custer, June 25, 1876

Ho-ka hey! It is a good day to fight! It is a good day to die!
—Crazy Horse, June 25, 1876

On May 17, 1876, the Seventh Cavalry left Fort Abraham Lincoln to the band fanfare of "The Girl I Left Behind Me." Although President Grant had initially forbidden George Armstrong Custer to take part in the campaign against the Sioux, generals Phil Sheridan and Alfred Terry had interceded on Custer's behalf. Grant was angry at Custer for testifying in a corruption trial of his secretary of war, and for publicly denouncing his brother, Orvil Grant. But the president relented under pressure from his generals.[1]

The military men were wary of putting Custer in charge of the Seventh Cavalry. General Sherman put it plainly in a telegram to General Terry, "Advise Custer to be prudent not to take along any newspaper men who always work mischief, and to abstain from any personalities in the future. Tell him I want him to confine his whole mind to his legitimate office. . . ."[2]

Custer immediately violated General Sherman's order

by taking along Mark Kellogg, a fawning reporter whose dispatches reached the *New York Herald*, to record his exploits. Apparently, Custer told his Indian scouts that this was to be his last campaign. After his expected victory in the Sioux War, a war that was being closely watched by the press and the public, George Armstrong Custer planned to run for the presidency of the United States.[3]

In addition to the Seventh Cavalry, on March 1 a large force of over eight hundred troops had left the North Platte region under the command of General George Crook. On March 17, 1876, Crook's soldiers, led by Colonel J. J. Reynolds, attacked a peaceful camp of Northern Cheyenne and Sioux camped near the Powder River not far from Crazy Horse. This was a pointless, cruel attack, for the Cheyenne leaders, Two Moons and Old Bear, along with Crazy Horse's lifelong friend He Dog (who led ten Oglala lodges), had decided to obey the government's order and return to the reservation peacefully. Now, with their camp burned and a number of dead and wounded, the furious remnants of the Northern Cheyenne and He Dog's people joined Crazy Horse; they too were going to fight. But the whites had left the field. Because of the still bitter winter weather, and the fact that Colonel Reynolds had many wounded, General Crook was forced to give up his campaign. He turned his large force back toward the Platte.[4]

With their warrior ranks swelling as never before, the Oglalas held an unprecedented council to decide on a new kind of chief. The Oglalas had never had a supreme chief for war and peace, and the unanimous choice was Crazy Horse, who was given the chieftainship for life. Runners were sent to the Red Cloud and Spotted Tail agencies, urging younger warriors to come north and fight with their new chief. "Come!" the runners said. "Crazy Horse leads us all!"

Soon the Oglalas were joined by Cheyenne and Sioux from many bands, who heard that Crazy Horse and Sitting Bull were gathering warriors to drive the whites from the plains. Even Red Cloud's son left his father's agency to join the great Sioux encampment preparing for battle. In addition to the Oglalas of Crazy Horse and the Hunkpapas of Sitting Bull and Chief Gall, there were the Sans Arcs led by Spotted Eagle; the Minniconjous led by Fast Bull and Touch-the-Clouds; Two Moons and his Cheyenne; and even remnants of the Santee, Yankton, Two Kettle, and Blackfeet bands of the Sioux Nation.[5]

This gathering of so many tribes, camped on the Rosebud Creek (a tributary of the Yellowstone River in eastern Montana), was a reminder of Sand Creek and Custer's decimation of the Cheyenne on the Washita. How many Indians were actually present for this last great encampment of the Plains Indians is impossible to estimate. Some historians believe there were two thousand lodges or more. This would mean that between two thousand and four thousand angry warriors were gathering for one last battle against the whites. An official of the National Park Service says the Indian camp "may have included between 12,000 and 15,000 Indians, probably as many as 5,000 being warriors."[6]

And for once, because so many agency Indians had joined up with the hostiles, almost half the warriors had guns. Although their rifles were not as good as the weapons of the soldiers, having guns gave the warriors confidence that they could match the enemy's firepower. With over ten thousand ponies, the Indians were also remarkably mobile and could move fifty miles in a single day, even with their women and children.[7]

The Indians' knowledge of the movements of the soldiers was far superior to the little information the soldiers gathered. Even if they didn't join Crazy Horse and Sitting Bull, many agency Indians were sympathetic. So they passed valuable information about troop movements and numbers to Crazy Horse, Sitting Bull, Gall, and other tribal leaders who had joined the opposition.

In early June, the Hunkpapa held their ritual Sun Dance in the Rosebud Valley, with their leader Sitting Bull taking an active role. The Hunkpapa mystic, medicine man,

In the early 1870s Custer posed with some of his scouts in the Montana territory. Kneeling beside Custer is his favorite scout, Bloody Knife, who would die with the colonel at the Little Bighorn in 1876.

and war chief was now the overall "commander in chief" of the combined Indian forces (he had been nominated by all the chiefs in a war council held in preparation for the coming battle).[8]

Sitting Bull had participated in the Sun Dance in the past and his chest and back bore the scars of many previous dances. This time, Sitting Bull allowed his adopted brother, Jumping Bull, to cut fifty pieces of flesh from his right arm with a sharpened awl and then fifty more from his left arm. With blood flowing down his arms the Hunkpapa stared directly into the sun and began the ritual dance. He danced for eighteen straight hours. On noon of the second day Sitting Bull fainted and saw the vision he had been seeking. Sitting Bull's vision was of bluecoated soldiers falling into the Sioux camp like grasshoppers, with their heads bent in defeat and their hats falling off. In his vision he heard the voice of "Wakan Tanka" (the Great Spirit or the Great Mystery), the Sioux god, say,

> These soldiers won't listen. They are like grasshoppers that have no ears. I give you these soldiers as a gift, because they won't listen.[9]

Awaking from his trance, Sitting Bull told his followers that they were destined to win a great victory and that the bluecoats would be crushed like insects. He said, "The enemy soldiers are gifts from the Great Mysterious. Kill them, but do not take their guns or horses. If you set your hearts on the wealth of the white men, it will be a curse on our nation."[10]

After the Sun Dance the Indians moved their encampment to the valley of the Little Bighorn, settling down along the banks of Ash Creek. On June 16, Cheyenne scouts brought news that they had spotted a large force of one thousand soldiers and 260 Crow and Shoshone scouts heading north under the command of General Crook, whom the Indians called "Three Stars."

Crook was coming at the Indians as part of a three-pronged attack. From Fort Ellis in Montana, Major General John Gibbon was moving east down the Yellowstone River with 450 soldiers. General Terry was moving up the Yellowstone with a force of 2,700 men. Colonel George A. Custer rode with Terry at the head of twelve troops of the Seventh Cavalry. With Crook's forces moving rapidly from the south, the object was to locate the Sioux camp, trap them, and overwhelm them before they could escape.[11]

The tactical leader for the Indians was Crazy Horse. Instead of waiting for the soldiers to reach their encampment, Crazy Horse decided to take the battle to the whites. Gathering a thousand Cheyenne and Sioux warriors Crazy Horse said,

> These soldiers of the Great Father do not seem to be men like you. They have no homes anywhere, no wives but the pay-women, no sons that they can know. Now, my friends, they are here in our country looking for us to kill. In this war we must fight them in a different way from any Lakotas have ever seen, not with the counting of many coups or doing great deeds to be told in the victory dance. We must make this a war of killing, a war of finishing, so we can live in peace in our own country.[12]

That night, June 16, Crazy Horse led a forced march from the Bighorn to the Rosebud Creek, about thirty miles away. The Indians marched in column formation with the Sioux and Cheyenne Akicita guarding the front, rear, and flanks to make sure that some hot headed young warrior did not ride ahead and put Crook on his guard before Crazy Horse was ready to attack. When they reached the west side of the Rosebud Valley, Crazy Horse crept to the top of a hill where he could look down and see Crook's 1,200 soldiers scattered on both sides of the Rosebud River. The valley would have been a perfect place to ambush Crook if Crazy Horse could draw him into it the way he had lured the hapless Fettermen ten years earlier. But by this time Crook and his Indian scouts were familiar with Crazy Horse's tactics. As Crazy Horse considered what to do, gazing down on Crook's position, a number of Crow scouts working for the army spotted him. Seeing the large number of Sioux and Cheyenne behind him, the Crows took off at full gallop shouting "Lakotas! Lakotas!" (Sioux! Sioux!) Crazy Horse's warriors could be held back no longer. They chased the Crows and the first engagement of the Battle of the Rosebud was under way.[13]

The battle was brutal and confusing as both sides engaged in fierce hand-to-hand combat with charges and countercharges. Crazy Horse led the Indian charges fighting furiously, his long unbraided hair flowing down his back. He wore a red calfskin cape with white spots signifying the hailstones of his long-ago vision. The cape flapped in the wind as he jumped from his spotted pony to fire at the soldiers from the ground. At one point Crazy Horse saw the Cheyenne chief Comes-in-Sight surrounded by white soldiers and about to be killed. The chief's sister, Buffalo Calf Road Woman, leaped on her pony and charged in to save her brother. The chief jumped up behind her and they galloped away under a hail of bullets. As a result, the Cheyenne would call the Rosebud, "Where the Girl Saved Her Brother." Crazy Horse remained in the thick of the fighting, urging his warriors forward and shouting encouragement: "Hold on my friends! Be Strong! Remember the helpless ones at home!"[14]

The battle was, despite its fierceness, inconclusive. Out of ammunition, with their horses exhausted from the long night march and the furious fighting, the tired and scattered warriors were ordered to withdraw by Crazy Horse. They headed back to their camp near the Little Bighorn. Later the Indians claimed they lost eleven warriors. Crook, who lost twenty-one soldiers and suffered more than twice that many wounded, claimed victory in his official report saying, "My troops beat the Indians on a field of their own choosing and drove them in utter rout from it, as far as the proper care of my wounded and prudence would justify."[15]

But if the Rosebud was a victory, it was a hollow one. For Crook was forced to withdraw from his three-pronged offensive and return to his base camp in the south. By seizing the offensive from Crook, Crazy Horse had removed one of the key military players and his forces from the field.

Even with Crook out of the picture, the other American forces continued moving toward the Sioux. As Stephen E. Ambrose wrote,

The truth was that every senior officer on the three expeditions—Gibbon, Terry and Custer—wanted a crack at the hostiles for himself. Each was convinced that no force of Indians, no matter how large, could stand up to their fire power. They all knew that this would be the last big Indian fight on the Plains and that the victor would become one of the Great Captains: his tactics would be studied in West Point classrooms and the nation would give him whatever reward he desired.[16]

General Terry and his troops moved up the Yellowstone River and set up their base camp at the mouth of the Rosebud on the steamer *Far West*. Early on June 21, Terry ordered Gibbon's column, which had moved down the Yellowstone as far as the Tongue River (where Miles City, Montana, is now located), to march back up the Yellowstone while he conferred with his senior officers on the steamer. On the afternoon of June 21, Custer, Gibbon, and other officers met with Terry to discuss their plan of attack.

Terry's plan was for Gibbon to go back up the Yellowstone, cross the Bighorn River, and follow that to the Little Bighorn River. In the meantime, Custer would lead the Seventh Cavalry up the Rosebud Creek and follow the Indian trail that had been scouted and reported earlier by Major Marcus A. Reno. Terry's goal was to squeeze the Indians between two fast-moving armies and force them to fight.[17]

General Terry wanted Custer to march toward the Indian encampment, and he offered to let Custer take his Gatling guns as well as four extra troops of the Second Cavalry. Custer, afraid the heavy guns would slow his march, refused the guns and the extra soldiers, even though they would have increased his fighting strength by 30 percent. Custer's written orders gave him freedom of movement, but he was not to start toward the Little Bighorn until Gibbon joined up with him for a joint attack on June 26. Terry wanted all his commanders in place before any serious fighting began.

On June 22, the Seventh Cavalry, numbering 611 men,

forty-four Indian scouts (mostly Crows and Arikaras), twenty packers and guides, and one civilian reporter, started up the Rosebud under the command of Custer. As he and his men paraded past generals Terry and Gibbon, Gibbon called out, "Now, Custer, don't be greedy, but wait for us." Custer smiled and called back, "No, I will not."

Communications being what they were in 1876, the generals did not even know where Crook had gone. Apparently, none of the officers in command that day on the *Far West* knew that General Crook had withdrawn from the field.[18]

That night Custer called a meeting of his field officers. He warned them to keep their troopers in rank and in order, not to allow any sport shooting, and to avoid unnecessary noise as they rode toward the Sioux encampment. In Custer's mind, surprise was required for success. Custer's own surprise would be that when he reached the Little Bighorn, Crazy Horse and about 3,000 very angry warriors would be waiting.

Although the thousands of Indians gathered at the Little Bighorn River were unaware that Custer and the Seventh Cavalry were approaching, the chiefs—Gall, Sitting Bull, and Crazy Horse—did know because their scouts monitored Custer's movements.

As the soldiers marched up the Rosebud, Indian signs were visible everywhere along the trail. The Sioux had even left the site of their Sun Dance lodge intact, with drawings in the sand of Sitting Bull's vision. Custer's Indian scouts anxiously explained what the drawings meant, but their fear failed to impress him. On June 24 Custer's column came to the point on the Rosebud where the Indians had crossed the stream a few days before. Trail signs indicated that large numbers of Indians had crossed the river. Still, Custer was unimpressed. He ordered a night march, which further weakened his exhausted troops.

On June 25 Custer's scouts looked down on the Little Bighorn valley, fifteen miles away, and saw a chilling sight. The valley below was dotted white with Indian lodges. On the prairie beyond the vast encampment was the largest herd of ponies ever assembled on the plains. When Bloody Knife, one of Custer's chief scouts, reported what lay ahead—more Indians than the soldiers had bullets—Custer smiled. When Mitch Bouyer, Gibbon's chief scout, told Custer that he had just seen the largest encampment of Indians in thirty years on the plains, Custer shrugged. He said the Seventh Cavalry would clean up the Indians in a single day.

Then Custer did something that military historians continue to debate: arriving at the Sioux encampment a full day ahead of schedule, Custer split his columns and divided his tired troopers. He had planned to rest his men for a day in the hills, but when scouts informed him that the Indians were aware of his presence, Custer decided to split his forces further and attack before the Indians could escape. Captain Frederick Benteen had command of three troops; Major Marcus Reno commanded another three; one troop stayed behind with the ammunition wagon, and Custer rode off at the head of five cavalry troops.[19]

It is difficult to understand why Custer would attack a large force of Indians without knowing how many he would face or exactly where they were located. But that seems to have been the case. Perhaps he did not respect their fighting ability; perhaps he was desperate for glory and worried that the Indians would escape and he would be denied the victory that the last great battle against the Sioux would certainly bring him. Whatever his reasoning, Custer's plan was to cut off an Indian escape down the Little Bighorn and attack the large encampment in three places.

He sent Reno to attack from the south, while Custer himself swung his troops to the north where they were hidden by a line of bluffs. Benteen was on the left flank. When some Indian boys discovered the fast-moving troopers and gave the alarm, Custer lost the important element of surprise by failing to launch a concerted attack at dawn as he had done in past campaigns.

At about 2:30 P.M. Major Reno crossed the Little Bighorn River to the west side and, with his three companies, began advancing. Reno was immediately amazed to see many more lodges and Indians than he had anticipated.[20] Although his orders were to charge, the size of the Indian camp apparently unnerved him. Instead, he ordered his men to dismount and deploy a skirmish line to fire at the Indians. Reno's attack, however, was a real surprise, and according to Oglalas who survived the battle, "[W]hen Reno attacked the Indians were almost uncontrollable, so great was their eagerness to press a counterattack, but Crazy Horse rode up and down in front of his men talking calmly to them and telling them to restrain their ardor till the right time."[21] Despite his efforts, hundreds of warriors rushed out of the village to engage Reno's troops and a fierce battle was soon under way.

Other accounts, also from Indian sources, indicate Crazy Horse was as surprised as everyone else when Reno attacked from the south. One recent Indian historian says that Crazy Horse was visiting with Cheyenne friends at the time of Reno's attack, and when he appeared, Reno's men were already retreating across the Bighorn River. As James Welch and Paul Stekler write in their study, *Killing Custer*,

> *Crazy Horse had not yet appeared on the field. Most of the fighting with Reno and Custer took place without him. But he was leading a large group of Oglalas and Cheyenne downstream to cross the river and attack from the north. When he did show up a short time later, the [Custer] troops were done for. They were completely surrounded, most of their horses had been driven off, and they found themselves on a naked ridge, vulnerable from all sides.[22]*

However, other accounts indicate that Crazy Horse was in the thick of the fighting. Lieutenant William H. Clark, who befriended Crazy Horse the following year and who interviewed him and many of the other Oglala participants wrote, "Crazy Horse rode with the greatest daring up and down in front of Col. Reno's skirmish line, and as soon as

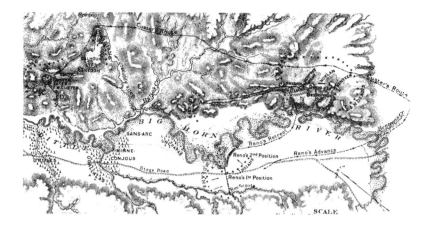

The Battle of the Little Bighorn, June 26, 1876. Custer divides his force and moves to the east side of the river. Separated from Reno and underestimating his own precarious position, Custer is overwhelmed by Crazy Horse and his warriors.

these troops were driven across the river, he went at once to Genl. Custer's front and there became the leading spirit."[23]

With hundreds of men and horses milling about in the heat, dust, and smoke of the Reno battle, it is not possible to give a full account of Crazy Horse and what he did. That day he rode his yellow pinto and was stripped down to a breechcloth, with the usual spattering of painted hailstones on his body and a streak of lightning down his face. He wore a red-backed hawk feather and, according to Mari Sandoz, rallied his warriors shouting, "Be strong my friends! Make them shoot three times, fast, so their guns will stick and you can knock them down with your clubs!"[24]

What is clear is the fact that Major Reno's failure to press his attack was the key to the day and when Reno was driven back across the Little Bighorn River, the Indians led by Crazy Horse and directed from the camp by Sitting Bull were then able to turn on Custer and his men. One of the few matters upon which the Indians agreed when they were interviewed in later years was the fact that Reno had caught them off guard, and that they were panic-stricken.

Had Reno followed through on his cavalry charge, these Indian eyewitnesses suggest that many of them would have fled. As one veteran cavalry officer later wrote, "I never could understand why Reno did not charge desperately on the Indians in front of him. His dismounting his men was against all sound military judgment."[25]

As Reno attacked, Sitting Bull hurried to his tipi to get his weapons. He was puzzled by Reno's tactic and feared a trap. "Look out!" he shouted to his warriors. "There must be some trick about this." But there was no trick and the Sioux warriors quickly mounted their ponies and rode out to meet Reno's force on the flat. Sitting Bull's Hunkpapa warriors made sure that their women and children were safe, and then they charged Reno's position from the west and north. Reno could see what looked like an endless number of Sioux and Cheyenne pouring out of the encampment, coming from every direction. He ordered his men to fall back toward the river. The rout soon turned into a slaughter as the Indians charged Reno and his panicked troops, riding down the fleeing soldiers. They brained the soldiers with war clubs; shot them on the run with guns and bows and arrows. As one Indian recalled, "We killed the soldiers easy; it was just like running buffalo. One blow killed them. They were shot in the back; they offered no resistance."[26]

From a nearby hill, Custer and his officers saw Major Reno was in trouble. They watched as the Indians attacked. Custer, however, didn't appear worried. Perhaps he expected Reno to get his men to mount and charge the upper end of the village. At any rate, Custer decided to take his five troops to attack the lower end of the village. Waving his wide-brimmed hat he called out, "We've caught them napping. We've got them."[27]

With Captain Benteen and his men off to the south (where there were no Indians), Custer barked an order to his trumpeter, an Italian immigrant who spoke limited English: "I want you to take a message to Captain Benteen. Ride as fast as you can, and tell him to hurry. Tell him it's a big village, and I want him to be quick, and to bring the ammunition packs." Custer's adjutant, W. W. Cooke, didn't trust the trumpeter's English and wrote out the following message, which has survived: "Benteen. Come on. Big Village. Be quick. Bring packs. P.S. Bring Pacs. W. W. Cooke."[28]

Then Custer and his men turned north behind the hills. At this point Crazy Horse sprung into action. Like the Indians in the camp below, he may have seen Custer waving his hat. Black Elk, who was only a boy, had killed and scalped a soldier that day. He recalled the shouts from those fighting Reno, "Crazy Horse is coming! Crazy Horse is coming!" After Crazy Horse was certain Reno had been stopped, he decided on the strategy that led to Custer's defeat. Instead of allowing Custer to sweep down the lower end of the encampment, Crazy Horse would ride out to outflank him. Crazy Horse called to his warriors, "Ho-ka hey! It is a good day to fight! It is a good day to die! Strong hearts, brave hearts to the front! Weak hearts and cowards to the rear." He then led over a thousand Sioux and Cheyenne warriors at a furious gallop through the camp beyond Custer's position. As he rode, more warriors joined him. His plan was to cross the Little Bighorn River and hit Custer from the right flank and rear.[29]

Custer still didn't seem to know that he was in trouble because he now made another error. He divided his command again, sending two companies to ford the river to test the strength of the Indian resistance. Custer himself took three companies east along the river, ending up on Calhoun Hill. The two companies sent to the river were met by the Hunkpapa chief Gall and 1,500 warriors. They blocked the soldiers from fording the river and counterattacked in force. With his divided troops now spread out, Custer must have realized that he was no longer on the offense. From defense, the battle quickly turned to one of survival as Custer headed for higher ground to wait for Benteen or even General Gibbon, due the next day, to reinforce his dangerous position. What he did not know was that Benteen's three companies had already arrived to support

Reno, who had lost a third of his command. They were dug in, desperately fighting for their lives.[30]

As Custer fought, with his remaining troops, up the hill to form a skirmish line, Crazy Horse and between one and two thousand warriors came up behind Custer at the top. Some scholars believe that by the time Crazy Horse arrived, Custer and his men were done. They were on a naked ridge, their horses had been driven off with their extra ammunition still in the saddlebags, and they were vulnerable from every direction. However, other scholars believe that it was Crazy Horse's next daring tactic that finally doomed Custer.[31]

The official government publication, *Custer Battlefield* describes this phase of the battle obliquely: "Much has been written about the Custer phase of the battle, but very few facts can definitely be stated."[32] But that is not the case. There were thousands of eyewitnesses to Custer's Last Stand on Calhoun Hill: the Sioux and Cheyenne warriors who were there. As Custer and his men turned to fight their way toward the top of Calhoun Hill that day, what they saw must have frozen them in their tracks: Crazy Horse, and between one and two thousand mounted warriors in full war paint, holding long battle spears and waving their Winchesters and other rifles as they whooped defiantly.

Crazy Horse and Custer were now no more than twenty yards apart. For an instant Crazy Horse looked down on Custer and his two hundred or so remaining hot and exhausted troopers, who were hard pressed by Gall's Hunkpapas on one flank. Did they see one another? "Long Hair" had cut his recognizable golden locks short for the campaign. So it is doubtful that, in the brief moment before the most controversial battle of all the Indian wars, the two men recognized one another in the smoke and dust.

The instant passed as Crazy Horse and his warriors, with terrorizing battle cries, swarmed down the hill killing everyone in their path. One Arapaho brave riding with Crazy Horse said, "Crazy Horse, the Sioux chief, was the bravest man I ever saw. He rode closest to the soldiers,

An Indian artist recorded his view of the battle of the Little Bighorn: Custer (center) lies slain among his soldiers as mounted Indians pursue the last survivors.

yelling to his warriors. All the soldiers were shooting at him, but he was never hit."[33]

In twenty minutes it was over. Custer and 225 members of the Seventh Cavalry lay dead in the late afternoon heat. Among those killed were Custer's brothers, Tom and Boston Custer, young Autie Reed, Custer's teenage nephew, who had come along to watch his uncle become famous, Custer's brother-in-law, Lieutenant James Calhoun (his sister Margaret's husband), and Mark Kellogg, the reporter along to help make Custer famous.

Custer's body was found stripped naked. He had a bullet through his left breast and another bullet hole in his temple (prompting speculation that he had committed suicide). Custer's body had not been scalped or mutilated, unlike those of many other soldiers, although some Indian women pierced his ears so that he might better hear in his next life. White Bull, Sitting Bull's nephew, was one of a number of Indians who later claimed to have killed Custer. He told a convincing story, credited by some historians:

> I charged in. A tall, well-built soldier with yellow hair and mustache saw me coming and tried to bluff me, aiming his rifle at me. But when I rushed him, he threw his rifle at me without shooting. I dodged it. We grabbed each other and wrestled there in the dust and smoke.... He drew his pistol. I wrenched it out of his hand and struck him with it three or four times on the head, knocked him over, shot him in the head and fired at his heart.[34]

Years later, Rain-in-the-Face claimed to have killed Custer's brother Tom, who had once arrested him at the Standing Rock Agency. Rain-in-the-Face became something of a "Custer's Last Stand" celebrity and made many public appearances. He told writer W. Kent Thomas in 1903,

> When I got near enough I shot him [Tom Custer] with my revolver. My gun was gone, I don't know where. I leaped from my pony and cut out his heart and bit a

*piece out of it and spit it in his face. I got back on my
pony and rode off shaking it. I was satisfied and sick of
fighting. I didn't scalp him.*[35]

What had happened? How had five troops of the elite
Seventh Cavalry along with their ambitious and dashing
commander been, as the Indians put it, "rubbed out"? With
Custer and his 225 troopers facing 2,500 warriors, was it the
sheer overwhelming force of numbers? James Welch an
Indian scholar, stated it succinctly:

*Custer, who had always relied on "Custer's Luck" in his
previous hell-for-leather battles in the Civil War and on
the frontier, had done everything wrong in this particular
engagement with the Indians. He had not scouted the
village or the terrain. He had seriously underestimated
the Indians' strength and resolve. He had not listened to
his scouts, who had pointed out time and again that the
village was immense. He had divided and weakened his
forces at every point along the attack route.*[36]

But there is also the generalship and military ability of
Crazy Horse. Before the battles of the Rosebud and the Little Bighorn, the Indians tended to ride in a circle around
their enemy, becoming easy moving targets for the expert
cavalry riflemen. After the Wagon Box fight, Crazy Horse
convinced the war chiefs to change their tactics. The Sioux
chiefs held their warriors back and, using Crazy Horse's
strategy, sent them in to attack and then retreat from several directions in waves against the soldiers. This attack-and-
retreat tactic fragmented the cavalry until they were forced
to fight in smaller units, more exposed to attack from various angles. It was the military skill of Crazy Horse that
helped the Indians emerge victorious.[37]

Historian Stephen E. Ambrose believes that if Crazy
Horse had not swung around, cutting off Custer's retreat to
the top of the hill, Custer could have held the high ground
and should have been able to hold off large numbers of

attackers. Ambrose writes, "Crazy Horse ruined it all. . . . [H]is real contribution to this greatest of all Indian victories was mental, not physical. . . . At the Little Bighorn, Custer was not outnumbered; he was also outgeneraled."[38]

At dawn the next day, June 26, the Indians were back on the attack against Reno, Benteen, and their troops. But the Indians, like the soldiers, were exhausted. Late that afternoon they set fire to the prairie grass in the valley and, as the clouds of smoke billowed above them, the Indians broke camp. The battle-weary surviving troops of the Seventh Cavalry watched with relief as the tipis came down and a long line of ponies and Indians moved slowly off toward the Bighorn Mountains. Reno and Benteen had lost thirty-two men killed and forty-four were wounded. The soldiers cautiously watered their thirsty horses and mules and started making cooking fires while they waited to be relieved by generals Terry and Gibbon. The Battle of the Little Bighorn was over.[39]

Under Sitting Bull, Crazy Horse, and Gall, the Sioux Nation had achieved its greatest victory. But winning a battle does not mean winning a war. For the Plains Indians, the defeat of George Armstrong Custer was the last victory. For the great Oglala war chief Crazy Horse, it was the beginning of the end.

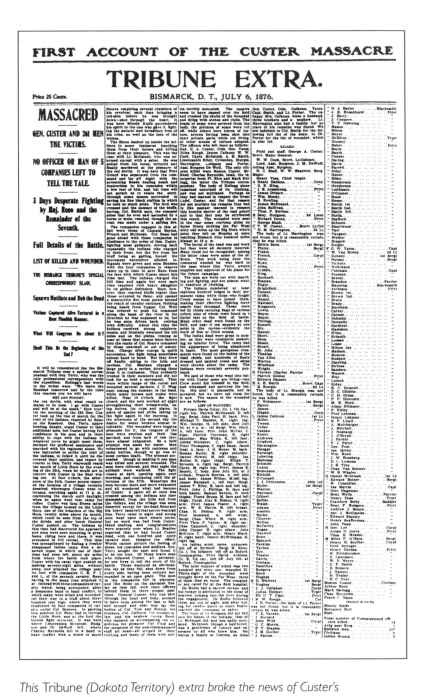

This Tribune (Dakota Territory) extra broke the news of Custer's disaster to a shocked nation.

CHAPTER TEN

THE DEATH OF
CRAZY HORSE

Let me go, my friends. You have got me hurt enough.
—Crazy Horse, September 6, 1877

It does not matter where his body lies, for it is grass;
but where his spirit is, it will be good to be.
—Black Elk, 1930

It was the week of July 4, 1876—the centennial celebration of the United States. As part of the nation's birthday party marking one hundred years of democracy and progress, people poured into the City of Brotherly Love for the Great Philadelphia Exposition, with displays of America's advanced scientific and technical know-how. But the country's national celebration was marred, if not ruined, as news spread that Colonel George Armstrong Custer and five entire troops of his Seventh Cavalry had been wiped out at the Battle of the Little Bighorn.

It was almost unbelievable and at first, when a Crow scout reached the steamer *Far West* to tell them what had happened, the officers dismissed his report—perhaps partly because the scout spoke no English. But the next day, one of General Terry's scouts, Muggins Taylor, arrived with the official dispatches.

Within days western newspapers displayed headlines

of the "Custer Massacre" to a shocked American public. On July 6, 1876, the *Bismarck Tribune* ran the headline "MASSA-CRED GEN. [*SIC*] CUSTER AND 261 MEN THE VICTIMS—NO OFFI-CER OR MAN OF 5 COMPANIES LEFT TO TELL THE TALE." The *Tribune* portrayed the soldiers as victims and the Indians who fought them as "red devils" and "screeching fiends, dealing death and destruction." The *Tribune*'s account was picked up by the eastern press and millions of Americans read the tale of the battle as told by writers who had not been there.[1]

As a Civil War officer, George A. Custer was not popular in the South. Yet in the heart of the Confederacy, the *Richmond Whig* waxed rhapsodic (and racist) in its eulogy:

> *The North alone shall not mourn this gallant soldier. He belongs to all the Saxon race; and when he carried his bold dragoons into the thickest of the last ambuscade, where his sun of life forever set, we hold him in the true spirit of that living chivalry which cannot die, but shall live forever to illustrate the pride, the glory, and the grandeur of our imperishable race.[2]*

In the West, grief was soon replaced by rage and the desire for revenge. In Sioux City a thousand men volunteered to fight, and Salt Lake City promised twelve hundred volunteers. In New Rumley, Ohio, where Custer was born, schoolchildren swore that they would kill Sitting Bull on sight. Senator Algernon Paddock of Nebraska introduced a bill calling for the extermination of the Indians.[3]

Only later, when cooler heads examined what had taken place at the Little Bighorn, were questions raised as to who was wrong and what mistakes were made. What was lost in the outraged reaction and the overblown military reports and press accounts is the important fact that the Indian response was a simple defense of hearth and home. As Black Elk put it, "Those Wasichus [whites] had come to kill our mothers and fathers and us, and it was our country . . . the soldiers were very foolish to do this."[4]

But President Grant had plans for the Sioux. Taking advantage of the national mood of hostility following the "Custer Massacre," the president quietly gave authority over the Indians to the military. On July 22, 1876, General Sherman was granted military control over all reservations in Sioux country, where he could then treat all the Indians, hostiles and "peacefuls," as prisoners of war. If the government could not get the Black Hills by hook, it would get them by crook. Armies under generals Crook, Terry, and Nelson A. Miles prowled the territory north and west of the Black Hills, killing Indians wherever they found them.[5]

Instead of staying together after the Custer battle, the tribes split into many bands. Scouts had brought Sitting Bull and Crazy Horse news that more soldiers were coming up the river—many more than they had fought with Custer, and they carried the heavy and much-feared "wagon guns" (cannons).[6] In August 1876 Congress added a clause to the Indian Appropriations Act that cut off all food and rations to the reservation Sioux until they agreed to turn over the Black Hills, give up all rights to hunt and roam off the reservations, and to allow passage through the remainder of their territory. Even though these Sioux had not participated in the Custer fight, the government was telling them to give up all their rights to their ancestral lands, or fight and ultimately die in battle, or starve to death.

The chiefs, including Red Cloud and Spotted Tail, were outraged. They and their followers had not killed Custer, yet they were being made to suffer as if they had. They spoke out against this new treaty which so shamefully violated the Treaty of 1868. But Red Cloud and Spotted Tail had more to worry about than honor. They were responsible for thousands of Sioux who would starve that winter if the government's goods were cut off from the agencies. So, after some posturing and angry words, Red Cloud and Spotted Tail, under pressure from yet another set of commissioners sent to treat with the Indians, signed the treaty. In December President Grant forwarded the agreement to Congress and on February 28, 1877, Congress passed the new treaty into law. With their precious Black Hills now officially signed away, the Sioux Nation ceased to exist. It had been passed into history by the signing of a piece of paper.[7] But there was still the matter of Sitting Bull, Crazy Horse, and thousands of hostile Sioux who would have to be brought under the control of the military.

After the Custer battle the Sioux and Cheyenne buried their dead—just how many Indians fell at the Little Bighorn has never been established—and headed west and southwest. That summer Crazy Horse returned to the Black Hills to lead several raids against miners and settlers but it was soon clear that he was fighting a holding action at best. Whites streamed into the region despite the danger of an Indian attack, and Crazy Horse knew that eventually his people would lose their land. Still, when he learned that Red Cloud and Spotted Tail had surrendered the Black Hills, Crazy Horse was furious with them for betraying their people. But he had little time to think about it because by late fall the north country was swarming with soldiers, and Crazy Horse was occupied with staying out of their way.

With Generals Crook and Terry back in the field with many more troops, the tribes went in separate directions to divide and confuse the soldiers. Crazy Horse and his followers went to Bear Butte, where he had been born. Sitting Bull and his Hunkpapas traveled to the lower Yellowstone. Other remnants of the great encampment were frightened and confused. Not wanting to be victims of the whites' desire for revenge, many Indians returned to their reservations.

On September 9, 1876, a detachment of Crook's cavalry attacked a band of Oglalas and Minniconjous at Slim Buttes, north of the Black Hills. The Sioux, led by Iron Plume (called American Horse by the whites), had just left Crazy Horse's camp on Grand River and were moving south to spend the winter on the reservation. Iron Plume was badly wounded in the battle and soon died. He had sent for Crazy Horse and Sitting Bull, but by the time Crazy

Horse arrived with some two hundred warriors, Crook had brought up 1,850 more men and taken the village. Crazy Horse's warriors fired on the soldiers, but with little ammunition and not much spirit for another fight, the Sioux withdrew. The next day, Crook retreated to the town of Deadwood to tend to his wounded, and it appeared that the Indians had fought the whites to a standstill. But the Battle of Slim Buttes was an indication of the future. Many Indians were slaughtered and the number of warriors that Crazy Horse and Sitting Bull could bring to a fight was rapidly diminishing. At the same time, the number of soldiers was growing larger every day.[8]

After Slim Buttes, the situation of the hostile Sioux under both Crazy Horse and Sitting Bull deteriorated quickly. As the plains weather grew colder, government armies began encircling the Oglalas and Hunkpapas led by Crazy Horse and Sitting Bull. In late November, General Crook collected an enormous force of infantry, cavalry, and artillery, with 168 wagons of supplies and enough ammunition to load on 400 pack mules. He swept through the Powder River country hoping to catch up to Crazy Horse, whose reputation was beginning to eclipse the better-known Sitting Bull as a Sioux war chief and leader.

Before Crook's troops found the elusive Crazy Horse, they attacked the Cheyenne. Led by Colonel Ranald S. Mackenzie, a force of over eleven hundred soldiers with four hundred enlisted Indian scouts (including some Sioux and Cheyenne who had surrendered after the Little Bighorn) surprised the village of Chief Dull Knife, killing many of his people and driving the survivors to take refuge with Crazy Horse.

In early December the Cheyenne found Crazy Horse and his Oglalas camped on Box Elder Creek on the Powder River. Crazy Horse and his band took them in and fed and clothed them. But the Oglalas did not have much themselves. With the buffalo nearly gone, game scarce, and living constantly on the run, life was hard for Crazy Horse and his followers.[9]

According to the Sioux who saw him that winter, Crazy Horse's behavior was more strange than ever. He walked silently through the village, speaking to no one; he could hear the children crying in their sleep, "The soldiers, mother, the soldiers!" He often left the camp to wander in the cold wilderness, alone with his thoughts. Many Oglalas worried about their leader starving or freezing to death. Black Elk's father found him once and Crazy Horse said, "Uncle, you have noticed me the way I act. But do not worry; there are caves and holes for me to live in, and out here the spirits may help me. I am making plans for the good of my people."[10]

Black Elk believed that Crazy Horse may have foreseen his own death and that he was making plans for the time he would no longer be there to help his people. Black Elk recalled, "He was always a queer man, but that winter he was queerer than ever."[11]

Crazy Horse was undoubtedly in great distress. After winning the greatest battle against the whites of any Indian leader in the nineteenth century, he had to watch in anguish as his people, facing starvation, ate their ponies and huddled in frozen lodges. His wife, Black Shawl, was ill with tuberculosis and it was, perhaps, at this point, that a saddened Crazy Horse made a decision. Stephen E. Ambrose says, "Crazy Horse decided to give up. . . . His responsibility was to his people, not to his own reputation. It was time to surrender."[12]

However, even surrendering was not easy. In late December Crazy Horse sent eight warriors carrying a white flag to meet with Colonel Nelson A. Miles. As Crazy Horse's warriors reached the fort on the Tongue River, a gang of Crow scouts attacked and killed five of them. Miles was angry with the Crows and sent them to Crazy Horse with tobacco and an apology. But Crazy Horse angrily refused the gift and rode away with his rapidly diminishing band of followers to face the worst winter in memory. Mari Sandoz wrote, "[W]hen Black Shawl saw the face of her man she went silently to strike her lodge for more wandering through the snow, chopping cottonwood for the horses, the men hunting buffalo for the kettle, everybody ready night or day to run from the horse soldiers brought against them by their own people."[13]

Miles finally attacked Crazy Horse with 500 soldiers on New Year's Day, 1877. While the women and children fled, Crazy Horse and his warriors fought a rear-guard action. However, Miles was relentless and hoped to add the famous Oglala war chief and his band to a list of conquests that would ultimately include capturing Chief Joseph and his Nez Perces, fighting the Apaches under Geronimo, and culminating in the last battle of the Plains Indians, the tragic massacre of the Sioux at Wounded Knee in 1890.

The fighting lasted for the better part of a week as Miles pursued Crazy Horse. After a fierce fight on January 8, Miles called off the campaign because of the severe cold and because he was convinced that Crazy Horse was beaten. Crazy Horse and his two thousand or so followers were capable of surviving the winter—but without food, more and more of his people would leave for the reservation. At first Crazy Horse tried to keep his people from leaving but slowly, group by group, they left. Although Crazy Horse found a small buffalo herd to keep his people going, the Oglala leader understood that he was finished. Even a visit by his old ally Sitting Bull did little to change the picture. The Hunkpapa chief urged Crazy Horse to join him and his warriors in fleeing to Canada. But Crazy Horse felt safe for the rest of the winter and refused.[14]

Over that winter the Americans sent Sioux emissaries to convince Crazy Horse to give up. In February, Crazy Horse's uncle, Spotted Tail, along with 250 warriors, were sent by General Crook to offer peace terms (which Crook lacked the authority to fulfill). Spotted Tail, who still led the Brulés at Fort Robinson, was a bitter rival of Red Cloud and now General Crook was a rival of Miles. It became a race to see who could bring Crazy Horse in first, with Sioux against Sioux as Crazy Horse was caught in a web of political intrigue of which he knew nothing. Years later Black Elk recalled Spotted Tail's search for Crazy Horse with great contempt:

> Spotted Tail, the Brulé with some others came to us. His sister was Crazy Horse's mother. He was a great chief and a great warrior before he went over to the Wasichus [white men]. I saw him and did not like him. He was fat with Wasichu food and we were lean with famine. My father told me that he came to make his nephew surrender to the soldiers, because our own people had turned against us, and in the spring when the grass was high enough for horses, many soldiers would come and fight us. . . . I could not understand this, and I thought much about it. How could men get fat by being bad, and starve by being good?[15]

Spotted Tail, however, couldn't find his nephew, and that April he returned to Crook only with the word that he had met with Worm, Crazy Horse's father, and that Worm had said that his son would come in to the Red Cloud Agency when the cold weather broke.

This was good news for Red Cloud, who was jealous of Spotted Tail's close relations with the army officers. In late April Red Cloud set out to find Crazy Horse and to escort him to the agency. For the first time in ten years the two allies of the Fetterman fight met out on the plains. Crazy Horse and his people were already on their way to Fort Robinson. As a token of respect, Crazy Horse spread his blanket for Red Cloud to sit down. Then he gave him his shirt as a gesture of surrender, one Oglala leader to another. Red Cloud reassured Crazy Horse and his lieutenants: "All is well, have no fear, come on in." But all was far from well. Crazy Horse, the greatest fighting warrior the Sioux Nation ever produced, was surrendering. He became, in effect, Red Cloud's prisoner.

On May 6, 1877, Crazy Horse formally surrendered to Lieutenant William H. Clark (called White Hat by the Sioux), the military commander of the Red Cloud Agency

Chief Red Cloud brought Crazy Horse in to surrender to white authorities in 1877.

that was located a mile from Fort Robinson. As so much else in his life, the surrender of Crazy Horse and his Oglalas was marked by drama.

Two miles to the north of Fort Robinson, Crazy Horse and his chiefs met with Clark. Crazy Horse extended his left hand and, through an interpreter, said, "Friend, I shake with this hand because my heart is on this side. . . . I want this peace to last forever." Then Crazy Horse, Little Big Man, He Dog, and other Oglala leaders, many painted for war, moved their entire band with their horses, dogs, and lodges toward the fort.

Crazy Horse was, as usual, dressed modestly without a warbonnet. With the exception of the Sioux who came out to greet him along the way, few of the whites who saw him knew who he was. He wore the single hawk feather tied to the back of his head and his long fur-wrapped braids hung down a plain buckskin shirt. He carried his Winchester across his lap. Behind the Oglala chiefs came the warriors, followed by the women and children. As the long procession of almost a thousand Oglalas and Cheyenne (300 families) moved toward Fort Robinson, thousands of agency Indians lined the route to get a glance at the now legendary war chief who, by his own defiance of the hated white authorities, had become their hero. For years he had led a hard but valiant core of "nontreaty" Sioux in their traditional nomadic life, living as truly free people on the Great Plains. The agency Indians began to cheer, chant, and sing for Crazy Horse as did the Oglala women and children in the line. Mari Sandoz wrote that "[A]ll the broad valley of the White Earth and the bluffs that stood against the northern sky were filled with the chanting of the peace song of the Lakotas." As one of the officers watched the long line of marchers through his binoculars he exclaimed, "By God! This is a triumphal march, not a surrender!"[16]

Without much formality, Crazy Horse surrendered 889 Oglalas, 1,700 horses, and 117 firearms for the promise of his own agency somewhere along the Powder River. But that promise, like many others, was never kept, as Crazy

Horse became entangled in a political struggle between the white authorities and the Sioux who were hungry for power. Of all the free Sioux, only Sitting Bull and his Hunkpapas were left.[17]

Life as an agency or reservation Indian was demeaning and difficult for Crazy Horse. He lived three miles from Fort Robinson, as far from the whites as he could, but he enjoyed little freedom. Once used to riding off hundreds of miles in any direction, he was now dependent on the American government for his food, clothing, and shelter.

Crazy Horse was something of a curiosity and many of the fort's officers wanted to meet the Indian leader who had beaten Fetterman, Crook, and Custer. He was also presented, by Red Cloud, with a second wife—the eighteen-year-old half-Indian daughter of a trader named Joe Larrabee. (Many Sioux had more than one wife.)[18]

Because of his fame, the American military leaders wanted Crazy Horse to visit Washington with Red Cloud and Spotted Tail to meet the president of the United States. At first, Crazy Horse refused, saying that he did not need to go looking for the Great Father. According to Black Elk, Crazy Horse said, "My Father is with me, and there is no Great Father between me and the Great Spirit." The truth is that Crazy Horse was intimidated by the idea of train travel, He had never ridden on a train, and he had many questions about his physical comforts, eating, and sleeping. Finally, he relented and agreed to the trip.[19]

But over the summer rumors abounded around Fort Robinson and the Red Cloud Agency. Red Cloud feared Crazy Horse and was jealous of his popularity among the agency Sioux. Red Cloud worried that Crazy Horse would become so powerful after a trip to Washington that the whites would make him chief over all the Sioux. He told Crazy Horse that the trip was a trap and that in Washington he would be put in chains and sent to prison. He also put out rumors that Crazy Horse was going to kill General Crook, and, with the younger warriors, leave the reservation and return to the warpath.

Because of these rumors, General Crook decided he would arrest Crazy Horse and send him to the desolate isolation of the Dry Tortugas, an island prison off the Florida Keys. Discouraged by his friends and his new wife (who may have been a spy for Red Cloud), Crazy Horse changed his mind and again refused to go to Washington for a meeting with the Great Father.

In the meantime, Crook's plan to arrest Crazy Horse was fueled by Crazy Horse's lack of communication with the American military authorities. Crazy Horse remained uncooperative, but he had no plans to dishonor his word and violate the peace even though—as he told Major V. T. McGillicuddy, the post doctor who had cured his wife of tuberculosis and who was his closest white friend—he had little affection for whites.[20]

That summer General Crook led an army campaign against Chief Joseph and the Nez Perce Indians. Many Sioux signed on to scout for Crook, while agency officials watched Crazy Horse closely to see what he would do. Crazy Horse didn't trust Crook and at first said that he would not help him. Crazy Horse was convinced the Crook expedition was a pretense to initiate a campaign against Sitting Bull, and Crazy Horse would have no part of that. Finally, after prodding from his friend Lieutenant Clark, he said he would accompany Crook to the Powder River and fight until there wasn't a single Nez Perce left. Unfortunately, the interpreter, for reasons of his own, purposely mistranslated Crazy Horse's words so that it seemed Crazy Horse had said he would fight until not a white man was left.[21]

The commanding officer of Fort Robinson, frightened by what he perceived as Crazy Horse's threat, telegraphed General Sheridan: "There is a good chance of trouble here and there is plenty of bad blood. I think the departure of the scouts will bring a collision here."[22]

Worried, Crook returned to Fort Robinson on September 2, 1877. He immediately called for a big council with the Indians. But Crazy Horse refused to attend, telling his people that he wanted nothing to do with Crook. Some of the chiefs who did attend told Crook that Crazy Horse was a desperate, and therefore dangerous, man. They also told Crook that Crazy Horse should be killed. Crook recalled the Rosebud defeat and the Little Bighorn. Like the chiefs, he too feared Crazy Horse. But he refused their advice and instead of having Crazy Horse murdered, ordered the chiefs to help with his arrest by the soldiers. The government planned to move all agency Sioux to the Missouri River and Crook knew that Crazy Horse had to be out of the way before this could be accomplished.

On September 4, the chiefs, led by Red Cloud, set out to arrest Crazy Horse, with four hundred agency warriors and eight full companies of the Third Cavalry—twice the force that had accompanied Custer at the Little Bighorn. But Crazy Horse, warned that they were coming, had gotten hold of two ponies and fled with his family to the Spotted Tail Agency.

For a while it looked like trouble. Crazy Horse's giant friend, the Minniconjou leader Touch-the-Clouds, and his warriors, lined up against Spotted Tail's Brulés. When the scouts chasing Crazy Horse arrived, the two groups traded threats and it looked as if Sioux would fight Sioux. At the last moment, Spotted Tail brought Crazy Horse out to the center of the parade ground to show that he was not harmed. Then, looking directly at his nephew, Spotted Tail made a speech to calm everyone down:

> We never have trouble here! The sky is clear; the air is free from dust. You have come here and you must listen to me and my people! I am chief here! We keep the peace! . . . If you stay here, you must listen to me! That is all![23]

That night, when things quieted down, Crazy Horse told Spotted Tail, Touch-the-Clouds, and the white Indian agent Lieutenant Jesse Lee that he had never threatened to harm Crook or to go back out on the warpath. Lee suggested that Crazy Horse surrender voluntarily and that he would see that Crazy Horse would have a chance to explain. Crazy Horse agreed but the next day apparently had second thoughts and told Lee that if he went back to Fort Robinson, "something bad will happen." But once again the agent convinced him to give himself up. That morning the nervous Oglala war chief made the forty-five-mile ride back to the fort accompanied by Touch-the-Clouds, Agent Lee, Spotted Tail, and a contingent of Spotted Tail's warriors.[24]

The party reached the fort at dusk and was immediately circled by thousands of Sioux, friends as well as foes. It was very tense and every witness's account is different. Even young Black Elk and other Sioux who were present did not know exactly what was taking place.

Crazy Horse was led to the adjutant's office, and the warriors parted to make way for him. His old friend He Dog rode into the fort bareback wearing his warbonnet. He Dog rode up to Crazy Horse and extended his hand, noting that his friend did not look well. Crazy Horse took his old comrade's hand as He Dog said, "Look out—watch your step—you are going to a dangerous place." Then Little Big Man, once one of Crazy Horse's most trusted lieutenants, grabbed Crazy Horse by the arms. This was the same Little Big Man who had ridden angrily into the center of the Black Hills Peace Commission threatening to kill any white who violated the sacred Sioux lands. Now, eager to show that he could be useful to the whites as a Sioux policeman, Little Big Man turned on his former war leader, jerking his arm and saying, "Come along, you man of no-fight. You are a coward!" Crazy Horse ignored Little Big Man but lunged at a Red Cloud warrior who called him a coward. Little Big Man, however, had Crazy Horse firmly by the arms.

Agent Lee then met with Colonel Bradley, the commander of Fort Robinson, and was told it was too late for talk. Crazy Horse's fate had been decided. He would spend the night in the guardhouse and would be shipped to Omaha the next day—the first step on his way to the Dry Tortugas.

Upset at being forced to lie to the great Sioux leader, Agent Lee told Crazy Horse that he was being taken to talk to the fort's commander. Little Big Man moved toward Crazy Horse, taking him by the arms, and led him to the post guardhouse. When Crazy Horse entered the foul-smelling jail he saw a prisoner's ball and chain—a dreadful sight he had glimpsed as a youngster. He realized that they were about to put him in a three-foot by six-foot cell with no windows and little air. Panicked, Crazy Horse pulled away from Little Big Man, drew a hidden knife, and cut his old comrade on his wrist. Knowing that his last hope for freedom would soon be gone, he turned and ran outside with Little Big Man right behind him. When the officer of the guard saw the fleeing Crazy Horse he shouted, "Stab the son of a bitch! Stab the son of a bitch!" Red Cloud, waiting in the large crowd outside the jail, was heard shouting, "Shoot in the middle! Shoot to kill!" Other soldiers were yelling, "Kill him! Kill him!"

In the melee, Little Big Man again grabbed Crazy Horse by the arms. As in his vision, twenty-three years earlier, he was being held by one of his own people. Crazy Horse made a desperate lunge to break free just as Private William Gentles speared him in the side with the bayonet at the end of his rifle. Then Gentles thrust at Crazy Horse again, stabbing him in the back and in the kidney. Crazy Horse fell to the ground, his clothes red with blood. As Little Big Man and a few soldiers reached to subdue him, Crazy Horse pleaded, "Let me go, my friends. You have got me hurt enough."[25]

The guards attempted to drag the wounded Crazy Horse back into the jail but the seven-foot giant Touch-the-Clouds stepped forward and gently carried his friend to a bed in the adjutant's office. Even at the end, however, Crazy Horse would have nothing of the whites, and told his friend that he preferred to lie on the floor close to the earth. To ease his pain, Dr. McGillicuddy gave him some morphine but there was little else he could do as Crazy Horse slipped in and out of consciousness. At one point, it

In a picture by the Indian eyewitness, Amos Bad Heart Bull, Little Big
Man and a soldier wrestle with Crazy Horse as Private William Gentles
spears him with his bayonet.

is alleged, Crazy Horse made a long speech to Agent Jesse
Lee absolving him of blame for what had happened. Lee
recorded Crazy Horse's words:

> My friend, I do not blame you for this. We preferred our
> own way of living. We were no expense to the govern-
> ment then. All we wanted was peace and to be left
> alone. Soldiers were sent out in winter. Then Long Hair
> [Custer] came in the same way. They say we massacred
> him, but he would have done the same to us had we not
> defended ourselves and fought to the last. . . . They tried
> to confine me, I tried to escape, and a soldier ran his
> bayonet into me. I have spoken.[26]

When his father Worm arrived with his mother, a gnarled
and wrinkled old couple, according to the soldiers who

Final journey of a great warrior

saw them, at first they were not permitted to see their son. Some accounts say that they did not see Crazy Horse until after he had died. But Indian accounts indicate that Touch-the-Clouds chased everyone out of the room and that Crazy Horse spoke with his father, whispering in a hoarse voice, "Ahh-h, my father. I am bad hurt. Tell the people it is no use to depend on me any more now—"[26]

In an hour or so, Crazy Horse was dead. Touch-the-Clouds told the Sioux gathered outside, "It is well. He has looked for death and it has come." Word quickly spread through the Sioux camp at the Red Cloud Agency. As Black Elk recalled,

> *That night I heard mourning everywhere, and then there was more and more mourning, until it was all over the camp. Crazy Horse was dead. He was brave and good and wise. He never wanted anything but to save his peo-*

ple, and he fought the Wasichus only when they came to kill us in our own country. . . . I cried all night and so did my father.[27]

Crazy Horse's parents brought a wagon and took his body away in a wooden coffin. Although Agent Lee wrote in his diary that he saw the burial scaffold not more than a half-mile from the post and helped erect a fence around the site, Crazy Horse's parents took his body somewhere out on the prairie to the north, past Pine Ridge, South Dakota. Some-where out there, no one knows where, Crazy Horse, wrapped in a buffalo robe, still rests.[28]

CHAPTER ELEVEN

IN SEARCH OF
"TASUNKE WITKO"
(THE STRANGE ONE – CRAZY HORSE)

They say, "Custer died for your sins." I say Custer is alive. We still have too many Custers and Mileses among the white people, but where is our Crazy Horse? One medicine man around here told me he had a vision that Crazy Horse would come back as a black man. That would be something.

—John Fire Lame Deer (1972)

Crazy Horse never drafted anyone to follow him. People recognized that what Crazy Horse did was for the best and was for the people. Crazy Horse never had his name on the stationery. He never had business cards. He never even received a per diem. . . .

—Vine Deloria, Jr. (1969)

There are two Crazy Horses. One belongs to the Indians. The other belongs to the whites. Neither Crazy Horse bears much resemblance to historical reality—to the man who actually lived.

The tendency among Native Americans has been to romanticize Crazy Horse. On June 26, 1995, the Cable News Network (CNN) broadcast a "Human Rights Symposium" to petition for the freedom of Leonard Peltier. Peltier, a Sioux convicted of murder at a 1975 Pine Ridge conflict between the federal government and a number of Sioux (in which two FBI agents and one Indian were killed), had been in prison for almost two decades. Peltier's lawyer, former attorney general Ramsey Clark (under President Lyndon B. Johnson), invoked the memory and spirit of Crazy Horse to remind the audience of the 119th anniversary of the Custer battle and of the role of Crazy Horse in that historic fight. Clark stated that Custer and his men had gotten what they deserved and that a year later, as retribution, "they murdered" Crazy Horse. He did not tell his listeners who "they" were.[1]

The legend of Crazy Horse began immediately after his tragic death. As the hard reservation life crushed the spirit of the Sioux and, in the end, the Plains Indian culture, that free and nomadic life for which Crazy Horse had fought passed from the American scene. As their way of life was destroyed, many Sioux replaced historical fact with myth as they recalled tales of the "old times" and the old battles. These stories were passed from parents to children and on to their children.

To the Sioux, Crazy Horse became a great hero and his life gave evidence of the injustices the Indian faced at the hands of the whites. Tales of Crazy Horse and his exploits, some true and others quite fanciful, began to appear. Some of the stories combined fact and myth, and as time passed it was more and more difficult to separate truth from legend.

Crazy Horse became, in many ways, a religious and spiritual figure who, like Jesus of Nazareth, was betrayed by his disciples and ultimately crucified for the sins of others. A Crazy Horse cult emerged among the Sioux (and other Indians) that caused some observers of Indian life, such as George Hyde, author of many fine books about the Sioux, to write acidly:

> It was evidently started among the Oglalas at Pine Ridge . . . aided by some white admirers of the Oglala fighting chief. They depict Crazy Horse as the kind of being never seen on earth: a genius in war, yet a lover of peace;

a statesman, who apparently never thought of the interests of any human being outside his own camp; a dreamer, a mystic, and a kind of Sioux Christ, who was betrayed in the end by his own disciples—Little Big Man, Touch-the-Clouds, Big Road, Jumping Shield, and the rest. One is inclined to ask, what is it all about?

Clearly, Hyde had doubts about Crazy Horse, whom he saw as a morose, sullen, and rather limited Sioux leader.[2]

Most Indians rejected the views of George Hyde and continued to see Crazy Horse as their hero. Some whites, however, demonized him after his death. To them he was evil incarnate—the bloodthirsty savage who, along with Sitting Bull, had decimated the legendary Custer and his heroic Seventh Cavalry at the Battle of Little Bighorn. To these keepers of the Custer flame, Crazy Horse was an example of frontier savagery who deserved to be obliterated from both history and historical memory.

Scholars, for the most part, avoided Crazy Horse and he rarely appeared in the readings and texts used in our schools and universities, except when reference was made to Custer, whose fortunes also rose and fell over time.

In the popular culture—in nineteenth-century dime novels, western adventure books, and even in films—Crazy Horse was usually portrayed as a stereotyped fanatic savage, even when he was remembered sympathetically. From the silent film *The Flaming Frontier,* to Cecil B. DeMille's 1937 epic *The Plainsman,* and the 1941 Errol Flynn–Custer saga *They Died with Their Boots On,* where Custer is killed in the last reel by Crazy Horse, there is no resemblance to his historical reality.[3]

In the shoot-em-up Technicolor extravaganzas of the 1950s (in *Sitting Bull* Indian actor Iron Eyes Cody portrays Crazy Horse as a fanatical war chief; in *Chief Crazy Horse* a white actor played Crazy Horse), the man depicted bears little resemblance to the real Oglala war chief.[4]

The first writer to take a serious look at the life of Crazy Horse was Mari Sandoz. She was born on the

Nebraska panhandle not far from the birthplace of Crazy Horse in the Black Hills. As a child, Sandoz heard endless stories from the Pine Ridge reservation Sioux who camped near the Sandoz homestead. She often visited Sioux tipis and played with Sioux children. Crazy Horse's old comrade He Dog, who called Sandoz "Granddaughter," and other Sioux who had known Crazy Horse, became her friends and often told her tales of their lives and of the old buffalo days on the frontier.

In 1930, Sandoz visited the Pine Ridge reservation with a friend, Eleanor Hinman. Hinman had conducted a number of interviews with Indians in preparation for a biography of Crazy Horse.

During much of the 1930s Sandoz and Hinman traveled the plains in search of Crazy Horse. Hinman turned over her research to Sandoz, who was a more accomplished writer. Drawing on many years of research and interviews and her intimate knowledge of Sioux life, Sandoz began work on a study of Crazy Horse that, since its publication in 1942, has become a literary classic—*Crazy Horse: The Strange Man of the Oglalas*. Sandoz was aware that she was reconstructing a major piece of American history. As she wrote to a friend, "The story is tremendous. . . ."[5]

The Crazy Horse Mari Sandoz presents is a figure of almost classical stature. A tragic and doomed man, Crazy Horse is shown with all the flaws and frailties of human beings. He is no superhero, but he is strange and extraordinary. Sandoz's Crazy Horse cannot survive against the overwhelming odds he and his people face. And yet, imbued with his sacred vision, he bravely does his best to defeat the whites, who would destroy his people and their way of life.

The Sandoz book has more merit as a literary effort than as straight history. Sandoz wrote in the lyrical and poetic style of the Sioux. Thus she transports readers across the wide sweep of the Great Plains and makes it possible to ride, fight, freeze, sweat, and weep with her Strange Man of the Oglalas.

In one of the most touching episodes in the book, Sandoz invests her strange warrior with immense humanity.
When his beloved daughter dies, Crazy Horse comes to her
death scaffold to mourn:

> *At the far edge were the trees and the scaffold with its
> little bundle. He knew it was the one, for on the posts
> hung the playthings his daughter loved: a rattle of ante-
> lope hoofs strung on rawhide, a bouncing bladder with
> little stones inside, a painted willow hoop. And on the
> scaffold, tied on top of the red blanket, was a deerskin
> doll, the beaded design of her cradleboard the same as
> on the dresses the little girl always wore, a design that
> came from far back in the family of Black Shawl. When
> he saw this the father could hold himself no longer. Face
> down beside the body of his daughter he let the sorrow
> locked in his heart sweep over him, the rickety scaffold
> creaking a little under his weight.[6]*

Historian Stephen B. Oates has observed that, "Sandoz's
empathy makes Crazy Horse a real human being, a man
who has feelings—fear, and grief—we can share. We are for
Crazy Horse, and this gives us a depth of understanding
we could never have acquired had the author treated him
disparagingly, or regarded him as only a name, a fact of history. Through Sandoz's empathetic portrait, Crazy Horse
came alive in our hearts as well as our minds."[7]

Beyond Sandoz, only historian Stephen E. Ambrose in
his fine study *Crazy Horse and Custer: The Parallel Lives of
Two American Warriors,* published in 1975, tells the story of
Crazy Horse with any level of depth and accuracy. In the
many books on Custer, the Oglala war chief usually makes
a bold appearance at the Little Bighorn only to retreat after
the fight back into the mists of Indian memory and shad-
owy history.

Because no photos of Crazy Horse exist, perhaps that
is as it should be. The myth grew that, unlike many other
Indian leaders who happily posed for photos, Crazy Horse

feared that his spirit would be captured by the large black boxes. The truth is probably simpler. Crazy Horse avoided whites as best he could off the battlefield. He did not like them and he saw cameras as tools of the whites. So Crazy Horse never permitted himself to be photographed.[8]

And yet no one who reads of Crazy Horse fails to have an image: we see him with his long sandy hair blowing in the wind, riding hard across the prairie, astride his favorite yellow pony with a single hawk feather tied to the back of his head. Painted on his face, with the small scar under his nose, are hailstones and jagged streaks of lightning. He is ready to fight and to defend the Black Hills from those who would drive out the elk, the buffalo, and the Sioux and Cheyenne.

In the Black Hills, not far from Custer, South Dakota, a statue of Crazy Horse is being carved from a six-hundred-foot-high mountain of granite called Thunderhead Mountain. The work has been progressing for years. A Boston-born sculptor named Korczak Ziolkowski was inspired by a letter from the Sioux chief Henry Standing Bear in 1939. The chief wanted Ziolkowski to carve a memorial to Crazy Horse and to all Indian peoples. Ziolkowski decided to make Crazy Horse the largest sculpture in the world and it became his life's work. Crazy Horse is mounted on horseback with his left arm outstretched and pointing. From the figure's shoulder to the tip of its index finger, the statue is 263 feet. The feather on Crazy Horse's head is forty-four feet of solid stone. Ziolkowski began the project in 1947 and worked on it until his death in 1982. His wife and children continue his giant project to this day. As one traveler to the monument and nearby museum remarked, "The Crazy Horse monument is the one place on the plains where I saw lots of Indians smiling."[9]

Mari Sandoz often heard a tale as she traveled the plains and reservations in search of Crazy Horse, a tale of how Crazy Horse's spirit still walked the guardhouse paths where he was killed at Fort Robinson in 1877 in his thirty-fifth year. Like others who became fascinated by Crazy

The artist's model of the memorial to Crazy Horse being carved in the Black Hills.

Horse, Sandoz wanted to learn everything she could about the life and death of the fabled Oglala war chief. She spent years looking for his burial place. The Sioux have long sought the final resting place of their hero; some may have found it and remained silent—to many Native Americans it is hallowed ground.

Who was Crazy Horse? He was a strange man and, even among his own people, he marched to a different drummer. He was determined to live his life the way he saw fit. He had little time for many Sioux customs and rituals and yet he was a deeply spiritual man. Like others who are different, he was little understood and many of his own people were jealous of his power or feared his popularity when he was alive. Yet, in his death, he became one of their greatest heroes. Many of the chiefs, such as Red Cloud and Spotted Tail, envied him or disliked him. Both have some responsibility for his death. Even his wartime ally Sitting Bull was puzzled by him.

Crazy Horse is not the mythical noble savage of a James Fenimore Cooper adventure novel. He was a real, and somewhat peculiar person, as his friends and relatives often recalled. And he was a fascinating man. He was self-less, a good friend to those he called friend, incredibly skilled as a fighting man, and either very brave or very foolish. Based on historical sources, one would have to lean toward brave. Like all human beings, he had flaws. He held fiercely to the nobility of his cause while, because of his contempt for most whites, making little effort to under-stand white Americans and the forces that drove them so relentlessly. He could be cruel and, like many Plains Indi-ans for whom warfare was a way of life, brutal. It must be remembered that, while many innocent Native Americans died on the frontier, innocent whites died in these times too.

What is often lost in any discussion about Crazy Horse is the fact that he was an individualist, a loner who would have scoffed at the Crazy Horse cult and the notion of hero worship. As George Roche has wisely observed, "Heroes are individuals. They come, one by one, each in [a] unique way."[10]

Crazy Horse was a master of his environment and could hunt, fish, track, ride, and shoot to survive. But with these survival skills, Crazy Horse did not survive; and although he won many battles, he did not win his war. There was great tragedy in Crazy Horse's brief life and in that tragedy lies the message that it is imperative to under-stand the times in which one lives. Crazy Horse shows us that no one is exempt from the forces of history.

Mari Sandoz never did find Crazy Horse's burial spot.

Finally, she realized that it was Crazy Horse's nephew Black Elk, the old Oglala holy man, who best understood the meaning of Crazy Horse's life and, perhaps, even his death. Black Elk told his friend John G. Neihardt, "Crazy Horse may be lying over there just a little way from us right now on Pepper Creek across that hill yonder. I do not know. It does not matter where his body lies, for it is grass; but where his spirit is, it will be good to be."[11]

Ho-Ka Hey!

NOTES

INTRODUCTION

1. Samuel Eliot Morison and Henry Steele Commager, *The Growth of the American Republic*, vol. 2 (New York, 1962), p. 137.
2. Mary Beth Norton, David M. Katzman, Paul D. Escott, Howard P. Chudacoff, Thomas G. Patterson, and William M. Tuttle, Jr., *A People and a Nation: A History of the United States*, vol. 2 (Boston, 1982), p. 447. Custer's middle name was Armstrong and, when the Battle of Little Bighorn took place, he was a colonel. The 1986 edition of the textbook corrected these mistakes (see vol. 2, p. 464) but did not enhance the role of Crazy Horse in American history.
3. Philip B. Kunhardt, Jr., Philip B. Kunhardt III, and Peter W. Kunhardt, *Lincoln: An Illustrated Biography* (New York, 1992), p. 34.
4. Wilcomb E. Washburn, ed., *The Indian and the White Man*, (Garden City, N.Y., 1964), p. 1.
5. Ibid., pp. 3–5.
6. Winthrop D. Jordan, *White Over Black: American Attitudes Toward the Negro 1550–1812* (Chapel Hill, N.C., 1968), p. 27.
7. Ibid., p. 91.

CHAPTER 1

1. Stephen E. Ambrose, *Crazy Horse and Custer: The Parallel Lives of Two American Warriors* (New York, 1975), p. 38, and Mari Sandoz, *Crazy Horse: The Strange Man of the Oglalas* (Lincoln, Neb., 1942), p. viii. The year of Crazy Horse's birth is disputed. Mari Sandoz, Crazy Horse's biographer, bases her facts on Indians who were still alive when she did her research in the 1930s

and who knew Crazy Horse. She believes Crazy Horse was born in 1842 although elsewhere in her study she places Crazy Horse's birth between 1840 and 1845 (see p. xv).

2. Ambrose, *Crazy Horse and Custer*, p. 38.
3. Robert M. Utley, *The Last Days of the Sioux Nation* (New Haven, 1963), pp. 6–7, Edward Lazarus, *Black Hills/White Justice: The Sioux Nation Versus the United States 1775 to the Present* (New York, 1991), p. 4, and Alvin M. Josephy, Jr., *The Indian Heritage of America*, (New York, 1968), p. 115.
4. Lazarus, *Black Hills/White Justice*, pp. 4–5.
5. Walter Prescott Webb, *The Great Plains* (New York, 1935), p. 53.
6. J. H. Parry, *The Age of Reconnaissance: Discovery, Exploration and Settlement 1450 to 1650* (Berkeley, Calif., 1981), pp. 29, 127.
7. Webb, *The Great Plains*, (New York, 1935) p. 57.
8. Lazarus, *Black Hills/White Justice*, p. 5.
9. Josephy, *The Indian Heritage of America*, p. 109.
10. Ambrose, *Crazy Horse and Custer*, p. 5, and Webb, *The Great Plains*, p. 43.
11. Laurence I. Seidman, *Once in the Saddle: The Cowboy's Frontier 1866–1896* (New York, 1994), pp. 63–64.
12. Webb, *The Great Plains*, pp. 58, 67.
13. Lazarus, *Black Hills/White Justice*, pp. 9, 11.
14. Ibid., pp. 9–10.
15. Ibid., pp. 10–11.
16. Ibid., p. 12.
17. Ambrose, *Crazy Horse and Custer*, p. 74.
18. Wilcomb E. Washburn, ed., *The Indian and the White Man* (Garden City, N.Y., 1964), p. 439.
19. Francis Parkman, *The Oregon Trail* (Philadelphia, 1931), p. 234.
20. Ambrose, *Crazy Horse and Custer*, p. 13.
21. Parkman, *The Oregon Trail*, pp. 89–92.
22. Ibid., pp. 101, 111.
23. Ibid., pp. 111, 112.

24. Ambrose, *Crazy Horse and Custer*, pp. 15–16.

25. Parkman, *The Oregon Trail*, pp. 204–205.

26. Ibid., p. 221.

27. Ibid., p. 226.

28. Ibid., pp. 269–270.

29. Ambrose, *Crazy Horse and Custer*, p. 17.

30. Ibid.

31. Robert M. Utley, *The Lance and the Shield: The Life and Times of Sitting Bull*, (New York, 1993), pp. 40, 45.

32. Lazarus, *Black Hills/White Justice*, p. 13.

33. Parkman, *The Oregon Trail*, pp. 272–273.

CHAPTER 2

1. Mari Sandoz, *Crazy Horse: The Strange Man of the Oglalas* (Lincoln, Neb., 1942), p. 3.

2. Stephen E. Ambrose, *Crazy Horse and Custer: The Parallel Lives of Two American Warriors* (New York, 1975), p. 38.

3. Ibid., p. 39.

4. Ibid., pp. 39–40.

5. Ibid., p. 42 and Mari Sandoz, *Crazy Horse*, pp. 17–20.

6. Robert M. Utley, *The Last Days of the Sioux Nation* (New Haven, 1963), p. 9.

7. Ibid., p. 10.

8. Francis Parkman, *The Oregon Trail* (Philadelphia, 1931), pp. 250–251.

9. Ambrose, *Crazy Horse and Custer*, pp. 42–44.

10. Parkman, *The Oregon Trail*, p. 147.

11. Ibid., p. 157, and Stephen E. Ambrose, *Crazy Horse and Custer*, p. 45.

12. Parkman, *The Oregon Trail*, p. 164.

13. Ambrose, *Crazy Horse and Custer*, p. 45.

14. Ibid., p. 52.

15. Ibid., pp. 52–53.

16. Ralph K. Andrist, *The Long Death: The Last Days of the Plains Indian* (New York, 1993), p. 17.

17. Ibid.

18. Lazarus, *Black Hills/White Justice: The Sioux Nation*

Versus the United States 1775 to the Present (New York, 1991), p. 14.

19. Andrist, *The Long Death*, p. 19.
20. Ibid., p. 18.
21. Lazarus, *Black Hills/White Justice*, pp. 15–16.
22. Ibid., p. 16, and Ambrose, *Crazy Horse and Custer*, p. 53.
23. Ambrose, *Crazy Horse and Custer*, p. 53, and Andrist, *The Long Death*, p. 20.
24. Lazarus, *Black Hills/White Justice*, pp. 17–20, and Ambrose, *Crazy Horse and Custer*, p. 56.
25. Ambrose, *Crazy Horse and Custer*, pp. 54–55.
26. Robert M. Utley, *The Lance and the Shield: The Life and Times of Sitting Bull* (New York, 1993), p. 44.
27. Ambrose, *Crazy Horse and Custer*, pp. 50, 56, and Lazarus, *Black Hills/White Justice*, p. 7.

CHAPTER 3

1. Allan W. Eckert, *A Sorrow in the Heart: The Life of Tecumseh* (New York, 1992), pp. 443–445.
2. Mari Sandoz, *Crazy Horse: The Strange Man of the Oglalas* (Lincoln, Neb., 1942), pp. 9–10, Steven E. Ambrose, *Crazy Horse and Custer: The Parallel Lives of Two American Warriors* (New York, 1975), p. 62, and Lazarus, *Black Hills/White Justice: The Sioux Nation Versus the United States 1775 to the Present* (New York, 1991), p. 21.
3. Sandoz, *Crazy Horse*, p. 10.
4. Ambrose, *Crazy Horse and Custer*, p. 63, and Sandoz, *Crazy Horse*, p. 13.
5. Sandoz, *Crazy Horse*, p. 14–15.
6. Ibid., p. 20.
7. Ambrose, *Crazy Horse and Custer*, pp. 60–61.
8. Lazarus, *Black Hills/White Justice*, p. 21.
9. Sandoz, *Crazy Horse*, pp. 23–24.
10. Ibid., p. 24, and Ambrose, *Crazy Horse and Custer*, p. 63.
11. Sandoz, *Crazy Horse*, p. 25.
12. Ibid., pp. 26–29, and Lazarus, *Black Hills/White Justice*, p. 22.

13. Sandoz, *Crazy Horse*, pp. 29–30.
14. Ibid., p. 32.
15. Ambrose, *Crazy Horse and Custer*, p. 65.
16. Ibid., p. 66.
17. Sandoz, *Crazy Horse*, p. 41.
18. Ibid, and Ambrose, *Crazy Horse and Custer*, p. 67.
19. Lazarus, *Black Hills/White Justice*, p. 22.

CHAPTER 4

1. Mari Sandoz, *Crazy Horse: The Strange Man of the Oglalas* (Lincoln, Neb., 1942), pp. 41, 105.
2. Steven E. Ambrose, *Crazy Horse and Custer: The Parallel Lives of Two American Warriors* (New York, 1975), p. 68.
3. Sandoz, *Crazy Horse*, pp. 43–44.
4. Ibid., p. 47.
5. Ibid., p. 60.
6. Ibid., pp. 63–64.
7. Ambrose, *Crazy Horse and Custer*, p. 69.
8. Edward Lazarus, *Black Hills/White Justice: The Sioux Nation Versus the United States 1775 to the Present* (New York, 1991), p. 23. Also see Ambrose, *Crazy Horse and Custer*, p. 71. Ambrose reports the number of Harney's troops at 600 although it hardly matters. If the Sioux had decided to act in concert against the Harney expedition, they had thousands of warriors and could have easily crushed the American force.
9. J. P. Dunn, Jr., *Massacres of the Mountains: A History of the Indian Wars of the Far West 1815–1875* (New York, 1886), p. 206.
10. Sandoz, *Crazy Horse*, pp. 69–70.
11. Ibid., p. 74.
12. Ambrose, *Crazy Horse and Custer*, p. 71.
13. Ibid., pp. 72–73.
14. Sandoz, *Crazy Horse*, p. 81.
15. Ibid., pp. 77–79.
16. Lazarus, *Black Hills/White Justice*, p. 24.
17. Sandoz, *Crazy Horse*, pp. 83–84.

18. Ambrose, *Crazy Horse and Custer*, p. 74.
19. Sandoz, *Crazy Horse*, p. 87.
20. Ibid., pp. 89–91.
21. Ibid., pp. 92, 98.
22. Ibid., p. 99.
23. Lazarus, *Black Hills/White Justice*, pp. 24–25.
24. Ambrose, *Crazy Horse and Custer*, p. 76.
25. Ibid., p. 77.
26. Sandoz, *Crazy Horse*, pp. 102–103.
27. Ibid., p. 103.
28. Ibid., p. 105–106, and Ambrose, *Crazy Horse and Custer*, pp. 77–79.
29. Sandoz, *Crazy Horse*, pp. 116–117, and Ambrose, *Crazy Horse and Custer*, p. 80.
30. Sandoz, *Crazy Horse*, p. 118.
31. Ambrose, *Crazy Horse and Custer*, p. 81.

CHAPTER 5

1. Alvin M. Josephy, Jr., *The Patriot Chiefs: A Chronicle of American Indian Resistance* (New York, 1961), p. 277.
2. Stephen E. Ambrose, *Crazy Horse and Custer: The Parallel Lives of Two American Warriors* (New York, 1975), p. 129.
3. Edward Lazarus, *Black Hills/White Justice: The Sioux Nation Versus the United States 1775 to the Present* (New York, 1991), pp. 27–28.
4. Ibid, and Alvin M. Josephy, *The Patriot Chiefs*, p. 277.
5. Lazarus, *Black Hills/White Justice*, pp. 28–29.
6. Ambrose, *Crazy Horse and Custer*, pp. 129–130.
7. Mari Sandoz, *Crazy Horse: The Strange Man of the Oglalas* (Lincoln, Neb., 1942), p. 127, and Ambrose, *Crazy Horse and Custer*, pp. 129–130, 134.
8. Ambrose, *Crazy Horse and Custer*, pp. 137–139.
9. Sandoz, *Crazy Horse*, pp. 134–135.
10. Ibid., pp. 175–178. Also see Ambrose, *Crazy Horse and Custer*, pp. 135–136.
11. Ambrose, *Crazy Horse and Custer*, p. 145.

12. Sandoz, *Crazy Horse*, p. 136, and Ambrose, *Crazy Horse and Custer*, p. 147.
13. Ralph K. Andrist, *The Long Death: The Last Days of the Plains Indian* (New York, 1993), pp. 79–80.
14. William Brandon, *The American Heritage Book of Indians* (New York, 1961), p. 345.
15. Andrist, *The Long Death*, pp. 85–87.
16. Ambrose, *Crazy Horse and Custer*, p. 150.
17. Andrist, *The Long Death*, p. 89.
18. Ibid., pp. 90–91.
19. Ibid., p. 90.
20. Ibid., pp. 94–95.
21. Alexander B. Adams, *Sitting Bull: A Biography* (New York, 1992), pp. 104–105.
22. Sandoz, *Crazy Horse*, p. 151.
23. Adams, *Sitting Bull: A Biography*, pp. 107–108.

CHAPTER 6

1. Stephen E. Ambrose, *Crazy Horse and Custer: The Parallel Lives of Two American Warriors* (New York, 1975), p. 154.
2. Ibid., pp. 156–157.
3. Alvin M. Josephy, Jr., *The Patriot Chiefs: A Chronicle of American Indian Resistance* (New York, 1961), p. 278, and Mari Sandoz, *Crazy Horse: The Strange Man of the Oglalas* (Lincoln, Neb., 1942), p. 189.
4. Ambrose, *Crazy Horse and Custer*, pp. 158–159, and Stanley Vestal, *Sitting Bull: Champion of the Sioux* (Norman, Okla., 1956), p. 128.
5. Ambrose, *Crazy Horse and Custer*, p. 160, and Vestal, *Sitting Bull*, p. 76.
6. Ambrose, *Crazy Horse and Custer*, p. 163.
7. Brandon, *The American Heritage Book of Indians* (New York, 1961), pp. 345–346. Also see J. P. Dunn, Jr., *Massacres of the Mountains: A History of the Indian Wars of the Far West 1815–1875* (New York, 1886), p. 373. Dunn reports that the war cost $35 million.

8. Ambrose, *Crazy Horse and Custer*, p. 163, and Ralph K. Andrist, *The Long Death: The Last Days of the Plains Indian* (New York, 1993), p. 99.
9. Edward Lazarus, *Black Hills/White Justice: The Sioux Nation Versus the United States 1775 to the Present* (New York, 1991), p. 32.
10. Ibid., pp. 32–33.
11. Ibid., pp. 35–36, and Ambrose, *Crazy Horse and Custer*, p. 226.
12. Brandon, *The American Heritage Book of Indians*, p. 366.
13. Ambrose, *Crazy Horse and Custer*, p. 228, and Lazarus, *Black Hills/White Justice*, pp. 35–36.
14. Andrist, *The Long Death*, p. 103.
15. Ambrose, *Crazy Horse and Custer*, pp. 229–230.
16. Ibid., p. 231.
17. Andrist, *The Long Death*, pp. 105–106.
18. Ambrose, *Crazy Horse and Custer*, pp. 232–233, and Andrist, *The Long Death*, p. 106.
19. Ambrose, *Crazy Horse and Custer*, p. 235, and Andrist, *The Long Death*, pp. 109–111.
20. Ambrose, *Crazy Horse and Custer*, p. 238.
21. Dunn, Jr., *Massacres of the Mountains*, pp. 422, 425.
22. Sandoz, *Crazy Horse*, p. 199.
23. Andrist, *The Long Death*, p. 117.
24. Sandoz, *Crazy Horse*, p. 200.
25. Dee Brown, *Bury My Heart at Wounded Knee: An Indian History of the American West* (New York, 1970), p. 136.
26. Ambrose, *Crazy Horse and Custer*, pp. 239–240, and Andrist, *The Long Death*, pp. 119, 123. Ambrose writes that the Indians had light casualties with only thirteen dead (ten Sioux, two Cheyennes, and one Arapaho). But Dee Brown in *Bury My Heart at Wounded Knee*, p. 137, says the Indians had almost 200 dead and wounded. Ralph Andrist writes, "The accounts given by the natives varied so widely as to be meaningless. One set the figure at only fourteen dead, another made it fifty or sixty, others agreed that about sixty were killed and at least a hundred of the wounded were so badly hurt

that they died later." Among the dead was Crazy Horse's close friend, Lone Bear, who died in his fighting companion's arms.

27. Ambrose, *Crazy Horse and Custer*, p. 242.
28. Brown, *Bury My Heart at Wounded Knee*, p. 137.
29. Ambrose, *Crazy Horse and Custer*, pp. 242–243, and Andrist, *The Long Death*, pp. 120–121.
30. *The Way West*, "The American Experience," Public Broadcasting Corporation, May 8, 1995, and Lazarus, *Black Hills/White Justice*, p. 39.
31. Andrist, *The Long Death*, p. 122.
32. Ambrose, *Crazy Horse and Custer*, p. 247.

CHAPTER 7

1. Cyrus Townshend Brady, *The Sioux Indian Wars: From the Powder River to the Little Big Horn* (Reprinted New York, 1992), p. 40.
2. John G. Neihardt, *Black Elk Speaks: Being the Life Story of a Holy Man of the Oglala Sioux* (Lincoln, Neb., 1961), pp. 86–87.
3. Ibid., p. 14.
4. Alvin M. Josephy, Jr., *The Patriot Chiefs: A Chronicle of American Indian Resistance* (New York, 1969), p. 284, Mari Sandoz, *Crazy Horse: The Strange Man of the Oglalas* (Lincoln, Neb., 1942), p. 207, and Stephen E. Ambrose, *Crazy Horse and Custer: The Parallel Lives of Two American Warriors* (New York, 1975), p. 259.
5. Edward Lazarus, *Black Hills/White Justice: The Sioux Nation Versus the United States 1775 to the Present* (New York, 1991), pp. 40–43.
6. Ibid., pp. 44–45.
7. Ambrose, *Crazy Horse and Custer*, pp. 276, 298.
8. Lazarus, *Black Hills/White Justice*, p. 46.
9. Ibid., p. 47.
10. Ambrose, *Crazy Horse and Custer*, pp. 276–277, 280.
11. Josephy, *The Patriot Chiefs*, p. 284, Ambrose, *Crazy Horse and Custer*, pp. 293–294.

12. Sandoz, *Crazy Horse*, p. 213.
13. Ambrose, *Crazy Horse and Custer*, pp. 299, 306.
14. Ibid, pp. 299, 306.
15. Laurence I. Seidman, *Once in the Saddle: The Cowboy's Frontier 1866–1896* (New York, 1991), p. 71.
16. Andrist, *The Long Death: The Last Days of the Plains Indian* (New York, 1993), p. 133, and Ambrose, *Crazy Horse and Custer*, p. 306.
17. Andrist, *The Long Death*, pp. 133–134, Ambrose, *Crazy Horse and Custer*, and Sandoz, *Crazy Horse*, p. 222.
18. Ambrose, *Crazy Horse and Custer*, pp. 332–333, and *The Way West*, "The American Experience," Public Broadcasting Corporation, May 8, 1995.
19. Lazarus, *Black Hills/White Justice*, p. 51.
20. *The Way West*, May 8, 1995.

CHAPTER 8

1. Mari Sandoz, *Crazy Horse: The Strange Man of the Oglalas* (Lincoln, Neb., 1942), pp. 225–226.
2. Stephen E. Ambrose, *Crazy Horse and Custer: The Parallel Lives of Two American Warriors* (New York, 1975), p. 331.
3. Sandoz, *Crazy Horse*, p. 226.
4. Ralph K. Andrist, *The Long Death: The Last Days of the Plains Indian* (New York, 1993), pp. 141–142.
5. Paul Andrew Hutton, ed., *The Custer Reader* (Lincoln, Neb., 1992), p. 3.
6. Ibid, pp. 103, 209, and James O. Gump, *The Dust Rose Like Smoke: The Subjugation of the Zulu and the Sioux* (Lincoln, Neb., 1994), p. 80.
7. Edward S. and Evelyn S. Luce, *Custer Battlefield*, National Park Service, Handbook No. 1 (Washington, D.C., 1961), p. 28.
8. Andrist, *The Long Death*, p. 159.
9. John Bartlett, *Familiar Quotations* (Boston, 1980), p. 610. This became the familiar frontier phrase "The only good Indian is a dead Indian."

10. Ambrose, *Crazy Horse and Custer*, p. 317.
11. Andrist, *The Long Death*, p. 161, and William Brandon, *The American Heritage Book of Indians* (New York, 1961), p. 347.
12. Gump, *The Dust Rose Like Smoke*, p. 81.
13. Andrist, *The Long Death*, p. 164, and Ambrose, *Crazy Horse and Custer*, p. 320.
14. Ambrose, *Crazy Horse and Custer*, p. 327.
15. Robert M. Utley, "The Celebrated Peace Policy of General Grant," in Roger L. Nichols and George R. Adams, eds., *The American Indian: Past and Present* (Waltham, Mass., 1971), p. 185.
16. Ibid., pp. 186–187.
17. Ibid., p. 192.
18. Sandoz, *Crazy Horse*, pp. 261–263, and Ambrose, *Crazy Horse and Custer*, p. 334.
19. Ambrose, *Crazy Horse and Custer*, p. 335.
20. Ibid., p. 339, and Evan S. Connell, *Son of the Morning Star: Custer and the Little Bighorn* (San Francisco, 1984), p. 69.
21. Sandoz, *Crazy Horse*, p. 241.
22. Connell, *Son of the Morning Star*, pp. 69–70, and Ambrose, *Crazy Horse and Custer*, pp. 340–342.
23. Sandoz, *Crazy Horse*, pp. 246–247.
24. Ibid., p. 254, and Ambrose, *Crazy Horse and Custer*, pp. 335–356.
25. Ambrose, *Crazy Horse and Custer*, pp. 381–382, and John Neihardt, *Black Elk Speaks: Being the Life Story of a Holy Man of the Oglala Sioux* (Lincoln, Neb., 1961), p. 87.
26. Gump, *The Dust Rose Like Smoke*, p. 73.
27. Brandon, *The American Heritage Book of Indians*, p. 366.
28. Ambrose, *Crazy Horse and Custer*, p. 374.
29. Ibid., pp. 375–376.
30. Ibid., pp. 362–367, Alvin M. Josephy, Jr., *The Patriot Chiefs: A Chronicle of American Indian Resistance*, (New York, 1969), p. 291, and Edward Lazarus, *Black Hills/White Justice: The Sioux Nation Versus the United States 1775 to the Present* (New York, 1991), p. 71.
31. Josephy, *The Patriot Chiefs*, p. 292.

32. Ibid., pp. 75–76.
33. Ibid., p. 292.
34. Ambrose, *Crazy Horse and Custer*, pp. 380–381.
35. Lazarus, *Black Hills/White Justice*, pp. 77–78.
36. Sandoz, *Crazy Horse*, p. 291.
37. Josephy, *The Patriot Chiefs*, p. 293.
38. Ambrose, *Crazy Horse and Custer*, pp. 387–388.
39. Ibid., p. 393, Josephy, *The Patriot Chiefs*, pp. 293–294, Lazarus, *Black Hills/White Justice*, p. 82, and Sandoz, *Crazy Horse*, p. 295.
40. Ambrose, *Crazy Horse and Custer*, p. 393.
41. Lazarus, *Black Hills/White Justice*, p. 82, and Josephy, *The Patriot Chiefs*, pp. 293–294.
42. Ambrose, *Crazy Horse and Custer*, pp. 395–396, and Josephy, *The Patriot Chiefs*, p. 294.
43. Robert M. Utley, *Frontier Regulars: The United States Army and the Indian* (New York, 1973), p. 246.
44. Ambrose, *Crazy Horse and Custer*, p. 397, and Sandoz, *Crazy Horse*, p. 301.

CHAPTER 9

1. Evan S. Connell, *Son of the Morning Star: Custer and the Little Bighorn* (San Francisco, 1984), pp. 104–105.
2. Ibid., p. 106.
3. Stephen E. Ambrose, *Crazy Horse and Custer: The Parallel Lives of Two American Warriors* (New York, 1975), pp. 405–406.
4. Alvin M. Josephy, Jr., *The Patriot Chiefs: A Chronicle of American Indian Resistance* (New York, 1961), p. 295.
5. Mari Sandoz, *Crazy Horse: The Strange Man of the Oglalas* (Lincoln, Neb., 1942), pp. 309, 311.
6. Edward S. and Evelyn S. Luce, *Custer Battlefield*, National Park Service, Handbook Number 1 (Washington, D.C., 1961), p. 9.
7. Ambrose, *Crazy Horse and Custer*, pp. 414–415.
8. Stanley Vestal, *Sitting Bull: Champion of the Sioux* (Norman, Okla., 1956), p. 143.

9. Richard Sheppard, "Sitting Bull Predicts Victory for the Indians," *Old News*, no date, pp. 5–6, and Vestal, *Sitting Bull*, pp. 149–151. The Sun Dance was a "coming of age" Sioux ritual that marked the passage of a boy to a man. It was very painful and involved piercing the breasts and being suspended from a pole. It was also a ritual utilized before going into battle. Many Sioux saw the Sun Dance as a mystical and religious experience.

10. Sheppard, "Sitting Bull Predicts Victory," p. 6.

11. Ambrose, *Crazy Horse and Custer*, pp. 418–419.

12. Sandoz, *Crazy Horse*, p. 319, and Ambrose, *Crazy Horse and Custer*, p. 423.

13. Ambrose, *Crazy Horse and Custer*, pp. 420–421, and Josephy, *The Patriot Chiefs*, p. 296.

14. Sandoz, *Crazy Horse*, p. 319, and Ambrose, *Crazy Horse and Custer*, p. 423.

15. Ralph K. Andrist, *The Long Death: The Last Days of the Plains Indian* (New York, 1993), p. 266.

16. Ambrose, *Crazy Horse and Custer*, pp. 424–425.

17. Luce, *Custer Battlefield*, p. 4.

18. Ambrose, *Crazy Horse and Custer*, pp. 426–427, and Josephy, *The Patriot Chiefs*, p. 298.

19. Ambrose, *Crazy Horse and Custer*, pp. 428–231, and Josephy, *The Patriot Chiefs*, p. 298.

20. Luce, *Custer Battlefield*, p. 11.

21. Ambrose, *Crazy Horse and Custer*, p. 438.

22. James Welch with Paul Stekler, *Killing Custer: The Battle of the Little Bighorn and the Fate of the Plains Indians* (New York, 1994), pp. 153, 168.

23. Ambrose, *Crazy Horse and Custer*, p. 438.

24. Sandoz, *Crazy Horse*, p. 326.

25. Cyrus Townshend Brady, *The Sioux Indian Wars: From the Powder River to the Little Big Horn* (New York, 1993), p. 239.

26. Vestal, *Sitting Bull*, pp. 161–163.

27. Ambrose, *Crazy Horse and Custer*, pp. 438–439.

28. Ibid., p. 439, and Welch with Stekler, *Killing Custer*, p. 156.

29. John G. Neihardt, *Black Elk Speaks: Being the Life Story of a Holy Man of the Oglala Sioux* (Lincoln, Neb., 1961), pp.

113–114, and Ambrose, *Crazy Horse and Custer*, p. 440.

30. Ambrose, *Crazy Horse and Custer*, p. 440.
31. See ibid., p. 441, for one view and Welch with Stekler, *Killing Custer*, p. 168, for the other.
32. Luce, *Custer Battlefield*, p. 12.
33. Ambrose, *Crazy Horse and Custer*, p. 442.
34. Vestal, *Sitting Bull*, pp. 169–170.
35. Brady, *The Sioux Indian Wars*, p. 289, and Welch with Stekler, *Killing Custer*, pp. 177–179.
36. Welch with Paul Stekler, *Killing Custer*, p. 166.
37. Ibid., p. 123.
38. Ambrose, *Crazy Horse and Custer*, pp. 445–447.
39. Luce, *Custer Battlefield*, pp. 20–21.

CHAPTER 10

1. James Welch with Paul Stekler, *Killing Custer: The Battle of the Little Bighorn and the Fate of the Plains Indians* (New York, 1994), pp. 189–193.
2. Edward Lazarus, *Black Hills/White Justice: The Sioux Nation Versus the United States 1775 to the Present* (New York, 1991), p. 89.
3. Ibid.
4. John G. Neihardt, *Black Elk Speaks: Being the Life Story of a Holy Man of the Oglala Sioux* (Lincoln, Neb., 1961), p. 131.
5. Dee Brown, *Bury My Heart at Wounded Knee: An Indian History of the American West* (New York, 1970), p. 302.
6. Mari Sandoz, *Crazy Horse: The Strange Man of the Oglalas* (Lincoln, Neb., 1942), p. 334.
7. Lazarus, *Black Hills/White Justice*, pp. 90–93.
8. Alvin M. Josephy, Jr., *The Patriot Chiefs: A Chronicle of American Indian Resistance* (New York, 1961), p. 302, Brown, *Bury My Heart at Wounded Knee*, pp. 302–303, Stephen E. Ambrose, *Crazy Horse and Custer: The Parallel Lives of Two American Warriors* (New York, 1975), pp. 452–453, and Stanley Vestal, *Sitting Bull: Champion of the*

Sioux (Norman, Okla., 1932), pp. 184–189. There is a major dispute here. Josephy says Crazy Horse came to Slim Buttes with 600 warriors. Ambrose says 200 warriors. Vestal claims Sitting Bull was the Sioux who led the rescue and that before American Horse died, he warned Crook that Crazy Horse would soon come but that it was Sitting Bull who actually came. Readers will have to decide for themselves. Sandoz, *Crazy Horse*, pp. 340–341, supports the point that Crazy Horse fought at Slim Buttes as does Welch, *Killing Custer*, p. 232. Welch reports the controversy on p. 307.

9. Welch with Paul Stekler, *Killing Custer*, pp. 237–239, Sandoz, *Crazy Horse*, pp. 345–346, Josephy, *The Patriot Chiefs*, p. 304, and Brown, *Bury My Heart at Wounded Knee*, p. 305.
10. Sandoz, *Crazy Horse*, p. 346, and Neihardt, *Black Elk Speaks*, p. 140.
11. Neihardt, *Black Elk Speaks*, p. 140.
12. Ambrose, *Crazy Horse and Custer*, p. 456.
13. Sandoz, *Crazy Horse*, p. 349.
14. Ambrose, *Crazy Horse and Custer*, pp. 458–459.
15. Neihardt, *Black Elk Speaks*, p. 142.
16. Ambrose, *Crazy Horse and Custer*, pp. 460–462, Sandoz, *Crazy Horse*, p. 361, and Brown, *The American West* (New York, 1994), pp. 238–239.
17. Ambrose, *Crazy Horse and Custer*, pp. 462–263, and Welch with Stekler, *Killing Custer*, pp. 244–245.
18. Ambrose, *Crazy Horse and Custer*, p. 463, and Sandoz, *Crazy Horse*, p. 379, and p. 381.
19. Neihardt, *Black Elk Speaks*, p. 145, and Welch with Stekler, *Killing Custer*, p. 247.
20. Ambrose, *Crazy Horse and Custer*, pp. 465–466.
21. Josephy, *The Patriot Chiefs*, p. 307.
22. Ambrose, *Crazy Horse and Custer*, p. 468.
23. Ibid., p. 470.
24. Welch with Stekler, *Killing Custer*, p. 249.
25. Ambrose, *Crazy Horse and Custer*, pp. 471–473, Evan S. Connell, *Son of the Morning Star: Custer and the Little*

Bighorn (San Francisco, 1984), p. 73, Sandoz, *Crazy Horse*, pp. 407–408, and Josephy, *The Patriot Chiefs*, pp. 307–308. Also see Neihardt, *Black Elk Speaks*, pp. 146–147, for the real sense of confusion that one gets from an eyewitness who heard Crazy Horse shout, "Don't touch me! I am Crazy Horse!"

26. Peter Nabokov, ed., *Native American Testimony: A Chronicle of Indian-White Relations From Prophecy to the Present 1492–1992* (New York, 1991), pp. 178–179.

27. Ambrose, *Crazy Horse and Custer*, p. 474, and Neihardt, *Black Elk Speaks*, p. 147.

28. Ambrose, *Crazy Horse and Custer*, p. 477, and Neihardt, *Black Elk Speaks*, p. 149.

CHAPTER II

1. Human Rights Symposium, Cable News Network (CNN), June 26, 1995.

2. Evan S. Connell, *Son of the Morning Star: Custer and the Battle of the Little Bighorn* (San Francisco, 1984), p. 75, and Ian Frazier, *Great Plains* (New York, 1989), p. 117.

3. Paul Andrew Hutton, ed., *The Custer Reader* (Lincoln, Neb., 1992), pp. 556–558.

4. *Hallowell's Film Guide*, edited by John Walker (New York, 1991), pp. 210, 1018.

5. Ibid., p. xi.

6. Ibid., pp. 285–286.

7. Ibid., p. xv.

8. James Welch with Paul Stekler, *Killing Custer: The Battle of the Little Bighorn and the Fate of the Plains Indians* (New York, 1994), pp. 116, 119.

9. Ian Frazier, *Great Plains*, pp. 115–117.

10. George Roche, *A World Without Heroes: The Modern Tragedy* (Hillsdale, Mich., 1987), p. 26.

11. John G. Neihardt, *Black Elk Speaks: Being the Life Story of a Holy Man of the Oglala Sioux* (Lincoln, Neb., 1961), p. 149.

BIBLIOGRAPHY

CRAZY HORSE

Ambrose, Stephen E. *Crazy Horse and Custer: The Parallel Lives of Two American Warriors*. New York: New American Library, 1975.

Josephy, Alvin M., Jr. *The Patriot Chiefs: A Chronicle of American Indian Resistance*. New York: Viking Press, 1961.

Sandoz, Mari. *Crazy Horse: The Strange Man of the Oglalas*. Lincoln: University of Nebraska Press, 1942.

THE PLAINS INDIANS

Andrist, Ralph K. *The Long Death: The Last Days of the Plains Indian*. New York: Macmillan, 1964.

Taylor, Colin F. *The Plains Indians*. New York: Crescent Books, 1994.

THE SIOUX

Lazarus, Edward. *Black Hills/White Justice: The Sioux Nation Versus the United States 1775 to the Present*. New York: Harper-Collins, 1991.

Utley, Robert M. *The Last Days of the Sioux Nation*. New Haven: Yale University Press, 1963.

NATIVE AMERICANS (GENERAL STUDIES)

Brandon, William. *The American Heritage Book of Indians*. New York: Simon and Schuster, 1961.

Brown, Dee. *Bury My Heart at Wounded Knee: An Indian History of the American West*. New York: Holt, Rinehart & Winston, 1970.

Josephy, Alvin M., Jr., *The Indian Heritage of America*. New York: Bantam Books, 1968.

Nichols, Roger L., and George R. Adams, eds. *The American Indian: Past and Present*. Waltham, Mass.: Xerox Publishing, 1971.

Washburn, Wilcomb E., ed. *The Indian and the White Man*. Garden City, N.Y.: Anchor Books, 1964.

MEMOIRS

Lame Deer, John (Fire) and Richard Erdoes, *Lame Deer: Seeker of Visions*. New York: Simon and Schuster, 1972.

Neihardt, John G. *Black Elk Speaks: Being the Life Story of a Holy Man of the Oglala Sioux*. Lincoln: University of Nebraska Press, 1961.

CRAZY HORSE, CUSTER, AND THE BATTLE OF THE LITTLE BIGHORN

Connell, Evan S. *Son of the Morning Star: Custer and the Little Bighorn*. San Francisco: North Point Press, 1984.

Hutton, Paul Andrew, ed. *The Custer Reader*. Lincoln: University of Nebraska Press, 1992.

Welch, James, with Paul Stekler. *Killing Custer: The Battle of the Little Bighorn and the Fate of the Plains Indians*. New York: Norton, 1994.

SITTING BULL

Adams, Alexander B. *Sitting Bull: A Biography*. New York: Barnes and Noble, 1992.

Utley, Robert M. *The Lance and the Shield: The Life and Times of Sitting Bull*. New York: Henry Holt, 1993.

Vestal, Stanley. *Sitting Bull: Champion of the Sioux*. Norman: University of Oklahoma Press, 1956.

THE WEST

Slotkin, Richard. *The Fatal Environment: The Myth of the Frontier in the Age of Industrialization 1800–1890*. New York: Harper and Row, 1985.

——*Gunfighter Nation: The Myth of the Frontier in Twentieth-Century America*. New York: Harper and Row, 1992.

Webb, Walter Prescott. *The Great Plains*. New York: Grossett and Dunlap, 1931.

INDEX

Akicita warrior society, 34, 35, 128, 144
American Horse, 80, 162, 163
Arapaho Indians, 72, 77, 83, 86, 87, 88, 93, 100, 104, 123, 153
Arikara Indians, 40, 42, 147

Battle of a Hundred Slain, 100–104. *See also* Fetterman massacre
Battle of the Little Bighorn, 146–57, *154*, 159, 160, 171, 178, 179
Battle of Slim Buttes, 163
Battle of the Blue Water, 66, 88
Battle of the Rosebud, 144–45, 171
Birth, 15, 29
Black Buffalo Woman, 70, 72, 78, 80, 127–29
Black Elk, 107, 108, 129, 152, 160, 164, 166, 169, 172, 175, 185
Blackfeet Sioux Indians, 15, 42, 43, 69, 141
Black Hawk War, 76
Black Hills, 15, 42, 67, 68, 69, 71, 88, 96, 115, 130, 132–138, 161, 162, 182, 183

Black Kettle, 84, 85, 87, 88, 121, 123, 124
Black Shawl (wife), 129, 164, 165, 170, 181
Bozeman Trail, 95, 96, 97, 99, 100, 103, 106, 111, 114
Bull Bear, 37, 124
Brulé Sioux Indians, 15, 25, 33, 38, 42, 48, 49, 50, 51, 52, 54, 57, 58, 62, 64, 65, 66, 68, 88, 91, 93, 98, 100, 109, 111, 115, 135, 165, 166, 171
Buffalo, 18–20, 23, 25, 27, 28, 33–34, 35, 43, 45, 62, 70, 71, 96, 114, 129, 130–32, *131*, 164

Cheyenne Indians, 38, 40, 67, 69, 77, 83–86, 87, 88, 89, 93, 94, 95, 100, 103, 104, 112, 123, 124, 126, 140, 141, 144, 145, 149, 151, 152, 162, 163, 168, 183
Chief Joseph, 165, 170
Childhood, 23, 32–58
Comanche Indians, 17, 123, 126
Conquering Bear, 42, 48, 49–51, 52, 54, 55, 57, 61, 62, 88
Crazy Horse (father). *See* Worm

Old-Man-Afraid-of-Horses,
    48, 51, 52, 53, 56, 61, 63,
    69, 90, 93, 110, 111
Old Smoke, 24, 37, 42, 43, 48
Oregon trail, 24, 25, 28,
    38–39, 40, 41, 48, 58, 61,
    62, 63, 75, 76, 82, 88, 93,
    95, 96

Parkman, Francis, 22–28, 30,
    33, 35, 36
Pawnee Indians, 17, 38, 51,
    61, 63, 82, 91
Powder River country, 42,
    77, 82, 95, 96, 111, 112,
    115, 118, 119, 121, 127–28,
    133, 138, 140, 163, 168,
    170
Powder River War, 94–106
    107–118

Red Cloud, 54, 69, 70, 78, 79,
    90, 93, 95, 96, 97–98, 99,
    100, 101, 102, 107–17, 118,
    121, 128, 129, 134, 136,
    140, 161, 162, 165, 166,
    167, 169, 170, 173, 184
Red Feather, 127, 129
Reservations, 110, 119,
    122–23, 125, 135, 137,
    140–41 155, 161, 162–63,
    165, 166, 169, 171, 175,
    178
Roman Nose, 93

Sand Creek Massacre,
    83–87, 88, 89, 94, 104, 105,
    124

Sans Arc Sioux Indians, 15,
    42, 69, 93, 100, 116, 141
Santee Sioux Indians, 15, 16,
    47, 76–77, 141
Santee uprising, 76–77
Sheridan, Phil, 115, 123, 124,
    132, 137, 138, 139, 170
Sherman, William Tecum-
    seh, 97, 106, 109, 111, 114,
    115, *116*, 119, 121, 124,
    138, 139, 161
"Shirt Wearers," 35, 77, 80,
    81, 88, 128, 130
Shoshone Indians, 40, 51,
    72, 75, 77, 119, 126–27,
    129, 143
Sihasapa Sioux Indians. *See*
    Blackfeet Sioux Indians
Sioux Treaty of 1868,
    116–17, 130, 132, 134, 161
Sitting Bull, 28, 42, 69, *92*,
    93, 94, 111, 117, 118, 133,
    135, 136, 138, 140, 141–43,
    147, 150, 151, 155, 157,
    160, 161, 162, 163, 165,
    169, 170, 179, 184
Spotted Tail, 33, 62, 65, 66,
    67–68, 88, 91, 93, 98–99,
    109, 111, 134, 135, 136,
    140, 161, 162, 165, 166,
    169, 171, 172, 184
Straight Foretop, 49, 50, 52,
    54, 55
Sun Dance, 43–45, *44–45*,
    117, 141–43, 147
Surrender, 159–76

Tecumseh, 46–48, 100